7 Keys to Freedom

Intuition

perception

will

memory

reason

MASTERMIND

Imagination

Will

Reason

Intuition

Perception

Will

THE ULTIMATE GUIDE TO DEVELOPING THE MIND

INTERNATIONALLY WRITTEN BY:
Gwen Boudreau, Canada ◆ Selwa Hamati, USA
Victoria Lazarova, Bulgaria ◆ Nita Matthews-Morgan, USA
Dawn R. Nocera, USA ◆ Alejandro Torres-Marco, Mexico

DNA International Publishing
Gahanna, Ohio

Copyright © 2012 by Gwen Boudreau, Selwa Hamati, Victoria Lazarova, Nita Matthews-Morgan, Dawn R. Nocera and Alejandro Torres-Marco
All rights reserved.

No part of this publication may be reproduced, distributed, or transmitted in any form or by any means, including photocopying, recording, or other electronic or mechanical methods, without the prior written permission of the publisher, except in the case of brief quotations embodied in critical reviews and certain other noncommercial uses permitted by copyright law. For permission requests, write to the publisher.

Published by: DNA International Publishing
Interior layout and design: Josh Matthews-Morgan
Cover design:

7 Keys to Freedom:
The Ultimate Guide to Developing the Mind

www.SevenKeystoFreedom.com

ISBN-13: 978-0-9885531-0-1 (pbk.)

FIRST EDITION
First printing 2012

Dedication

Special thanks to our families and friends for their abundant support and nourishing love.

We dedicate this book to Napoleon Hill, the greatest motivational author and teacher on the Principles of Success, and to Bob Proctor, one of today's living masters of Mind Potential.

SEVEN: About the Authors

"No two minds ever come together without, thereby, creating a third, invisible, intangible force which may be likened to a third mind."
~ Napoleon Hill

Six of us came together as a group of minds in the spirit of harmony with one purpose: To have FUN as we INSPIRE corporations of the world and our global community to reconnect with Spirit, experience LOVE, and create ABUNDANCE in all areas of their lives as we have and to openly invite them to join us as LUMINARIES HEALING our world.

Although there are only six of us — Gwen Boudreau, Selwa Hamati, Victoria Lazarova, Nita Matthews-Morgan, Dawn Nocera and Alejandro Torres-Marco — we call ourselves SEVEN. It is clear to us that soon after forming our group and formulating a common purpose, that we had created a true mastermind.

The Seventh Universal Mind is the real hero of this book, accessed only by joining of the 6 other minds in the spirit of cooperation and harmony. The Seventh Mind took over in times of doubt and worry and lead the way towards the ultimate freedom, freedom from fear. Only through accessing this Seventh Mind were we able to trust that our book, *7 Keys to Freedom*, would safely reach your hands.

Table of Contents

Foreword 10

Introduction 13

Chapter 1: The Mind 18
    By Selwa Hamati

Chapter 2: Your Imagination 31
    By Gwen Boudreau

Chapter 3: Your Memory 56
    By Nita Matthews-Morgan

Chapter 4: Your Reason 81
    By Alejandro Torres-Marco

Chapter 5: Your Perception 113
    By Victoria Lazarova

Chapter 6: Your Intuition 138
    By Dawn R. Nocera

Chapter 7: Your Will 158
    By Dawn R. Nocera and SEVEN

Chapter 8: The Mastermind 178
    By Nita Matthews-Morgan and SEVEN

Chapter 9: Your Awareness 190
    By Nita Matthews-Morgan and SEVEN

Author Bios 205

References 212

Foreword

"The intuitive mind is a sacred gift. The rational mind is an obedient servant. We have created a society where we honor the servant and have forgotten the gift."

~ Albert Einstein

What you are about to read in this book is information that very few people understand. It's information about you, your next-door neighbor, your mother, your son or your daughter. It's information about us as a people, and unfortunately, it's information that, up to this time, has only been exposed to a very select few. Read this book carefully. In fact, you may end up reading the book fifty times, and then you'll understand what author L. Ron Hubbard meant when he said, "If you read a good book through the second time, you won't see something in it that you didn't see before, you'll see something in yourself that wasn't there before."

Now, let's get busy. The area of the mind Albert Einstein referred to as the "intuitive mind" is the part of the mind that separates us from all of the animal kingdom — our conscious mind. All of the rest of the little creatures on the planet are completely at home in their environment. They blend in. They operate by instinct, sub-consciously. You and I are totally disoriented in our environment, and that is because we have been blessed with intellectual faculties that enable us to create our own environment. We have been gifted with these marvelous faculties — imagination, reason, memory, perception, intuition, and the will — and they are what qualify you and me as God's highest form of creation. These special gifts hook us up to our "inner world," that world which exists in our mind the same way our senses hook us up to our physical world.

We are programmed to live through our senses, through what we can see, hear, smell, taste, and touch. And we are conditioned to permit the outside world to dictate our mental state or the direction of our life. It's what we're taught from the moment we arrive on planet Earth. We have been convinced that what we can see, hear, smell, taste, and touch is all there is, even although all the great teachers of the past clearly tell us to go within, to live from the inside out.

Consider this. Think of the number of times you heard one of your classmates, or possibly yourself, being chastised for not paying attention in school. This incident may have landed you in detention or a spot in the corner where you were asked to stand for a period of time until the teacher felt you were ready to obey instructions and pay attention to what was being taught. Little did the teacher know that you were merely exercising one of your highest intellectual faculties, of imagination, to transport yourself to a more interesting environment than the one in which you found yourself, trapped.

Sadly, we go through our formative years without knowing anything of our mental faculties, or how to develop them to bring our genius to the surface, to allow us to express our uniqueness as a creative being. Fortunately, this book will help break that cycle of ignorance and provide you with sound information that will help you greatly improve the quality of your life.

The *7 Keys to Freedom* has been written by a group of individuals who have a sincere desire to make us aware of how to begin using our higher faculties so that we can begin living as God meant us to live. They have done an excellent job. I congratulate them for the time, effort, and care that have gone into the preparation of this book.

As you go from chapter to chapter, you'll begin to understand how to employ your higher faculties to create, in your mind, the life you dream of living. You'll be shown how you can manifest in your outside world a replica of that dream.

The effort that has been invested in creating this book touches me deeply. It deals with a subject I have studied for over fifty years and have actively taught all over the world. The authors of *7 Keys to Freedom* are students of mine who met a number of years ago while attending a special program my company conducts to train individuals in the field of personal development.

As you work your way through the book, you will see they have learned their lessons well. Needless to say, I am very proud of them and the great work they have done and are doing. When they approached me to write the foreword of their collective efforts, I was touched and quickly accepted the honor.

The entirety of this book is dedicated to a very serious subject that, when properly understood, can change your life for the better, forever. It deals with the uniqueness of you! The authors share their individual and combined efforts ... you will not only read but be privy to the age-old wisdom that has impacted their lives, that they now openly share with you.

Open your mind and read from cover to cover. Then, choose one of the higher faculties that perhaps piques your interest most and focus on it for 90 days. Then, continue in the same manner with each faculty until you have completed the book. You will be amazed and delighted with how you will be rewarded for your efforts. Perfection lies deep within you. Every faculty mentioned in this book can be strengthened and merely requires exercise. The more you exercise your higher faculties, the more effective you become. You have your homework cut out for you.

You have infinite potential locked up within, just waiting to be utilized; there is no limit to the success you can enjoy. Begin your exciting journey fully expecting wonderful things to happen with constant regularity. And always keep in mind that when it comes to personal growth, there is no finish line. Every aspect of your life can get better — and better is a nice word.

Bob Proctor
Best-selling author of *You Were Born Rich*
and Teacher in *The Secret*

Introduction

What is an Intellectual Faculty?

Can you remember the first time you really thought for yourself? A defining moment such as this either moves us forward into growth or keeps our feet firmly planted on the ground, unable to move forward and grow, and unable to think for ourselves. Imagine the world if Bill Gates had accepted the fact that he did not actually have a product to sell to IBM and, instead of creating DOS (the first widely installed computer operating system) with the resources he had, walked away in defeat. Gates thought differently about his life; he thought about what was possible and what he was capable of achieving. People like Bill Gates and the late Steve Jobs both thought of possibilities, not limitations, which is why they are, and were, considered leaders in their profession. Leaders choose to use their mind in a way that opens doors for them. In its simplest form, this unique type of thinking is "thinking for yourself."

Think of the times in your own life when you have achieved success. You used your mind in a way that separated you from the naysayers and the people who said it could not be done. Thinking for yourself is more than an occasional activity; it is the acquired habit of a natural winner in life, and it allows you to have doors fly open as you walk confidently forward on your life's journey. Yet how many people think and apply their thoughts on a day-to-day basis?

Dr. J.B. Rhine of Duke University declared, "Your mind is the greatest power in all creation." You interpret the world around you according to how you see it with your mind's eye. Imagine that your mind is equipped with mental muscles, just as your body is equipped with physical muscles. You already know how to develop your body's physical muscles through exercise; to develop your mind, you need to develop your "mental muscles," which we call here your "intellectual faculties." These intellectual faculties are imagination, memory, reason, perception, intuition, and will. Just as you can use your muscles in your body, either automatically or purposefully, you can also use your intellectual faculties without thinking (automatically) or purposefully. Thinking for yourself happens when you use your mind the way it was meant to be used: creatively, and with enthusiasm for your current life and the life you are creating.

This book will help you understand how your mind works so you can begin to use your intellectual faculties more effectively (purposefully) — and in doing so, find freedom in all areas of your life. We talk about freedom in life because it is not limited or shaped by anybody. Freedom is what *you* decide. It is *your* freedom. The ultimate freedom has always been the freedom to think for yourself in a way that creates peace of mind as you live the life you choose to live. Bob Proctor says, "If I'm going to be free, I've got to be me. Not the me you think I should be, or the me my kids think I should be. If I'm going to be free, I've got to be the me I want to be!"

Everyone is equipped with intellectual faculties. We are born with them — and still only a small percentage of the population effectively employ their faculties in a way that enables them to make a better life for themselves and the ones they love. This is why the same small percentage of the population earns the most money.

Your mind is always busy, but don't confuse mental activity with thinking. You have hundreds and even thousands of thoughts going through your mind every day; you must sift through these thoughts and purposefully direct them in a way that enables you to become the best you can be, regardless of your current resources or circumstances. If we let our thoughts run wild and uncontrolled by not using our ability to think *on purpose,* as we often do, then we are simply allowing somebody else's thoughts to take over our mind. Part of the reason for this is that we often misunderstand the difference between mental activity and thinking. You may have gone to some of the finest universities in the world or attended workshops and seminars to improve your life or professional skills, and still know little about your ability to think.

Introduction

Since we were small children, we have been programmed to value our knowledge of a certain subject according to a grade given to us, but we have not given any conscious attention to the importance of how we think and process this knowledge in our mind. We both enjoy and suffer from our thoughts. We are not aware of how we think or how to manage our thinking to enjoy a positive mental state and positive results in our lives. The awareness of how you really think will help you create a process for using your mind in an orderly way. The importance of understanding and mastering this process is crucial for your life. It is the real cause for every result and circumstance around you.

"We think in secret and it comes to pass, environment is but our looking glass." ~James Allen, As a Man Thinketh

Active, creative, and focused thinking requires applied knowledge and heightened awareness. Understanding your intellectual faculties is your first step toward that applied knowledge and heightened awareness. Once you become aware of why you do what you do, and why you interpret things the way you do, you begin to take responsibility for your life and to free yourself from the expectations of others. Each one of us has a desire to seek freedom, and an individual with awareness seeks freedom through the ability to think independently. That desire to seek freedom is what led us to the creation of this book.

You hold in your hands the "how-to" book on thinking for yourself. The ideas in this book can help you enjoy an abundant and happy life. Most people are not aware that their freedom in life comes from their ability to think independently. Only a few individuals grasp this idea, and the ones who do understand it stand out significantly because of their accomplishments.

Our thinking determines the circumstances in our lives. Sometimes we cannot change the facts and circumstances, but we can always choose the way we respond to them. We can determine how much power we allow them to have over our lives.

In this book, we will talk a lot about thinking, so that you can fully understand the process you use when you think. You will understand the tools and mechanisms you unconsciously use while you mentally process information. This information will help you choose and create thoughts that lead to your desired outcomes. We sincerely wish that you will discover your ability to think by developing the intellectual faculties of your mind and to start thinking with definite purpose. In doing so, you will fill your life with purpose-driven thoughts, habits, and actions, thus creating new results, which will give you your desired freedom.

All great leaders in the world agree on one thing: We become what we think about. For that reason, we need to master our thinking. We can harness the power of our thoughts when we master our thinking by using our intellectual faculties to create our life from the inside out, instead of living as victims of our circumstances and accepting everything from the outside in. Our intellectual faculties are like tools in a tool box, which we use to build our life, a set of keys that open doors to freedom and independent thinking. If we want to be more, do more, have more, and enjoy more of this life, we need to allow ourselves to change the thinking and logic that produced our current results. The great Albert Einstein said, "Logic can take you from A to B; imagination can take you anywhere." We all would like the freedom to think for ourselves so we can create what we want. When we have this freedom, we stop competing and start creating; we stop blaming and reacting to circumstances and start responding to them; we stop complaining about what we do not have and start creating what we desire; we stop fighting with ourselves and start appreciating who we are; we stop judging people and start accepting them; we cease not knowing what we want out of life and we start to make decisions and choices that focus on our desires.

When you use your mind to think independently, you will become increasingly aware of your unlimited potential. You deserve to enjoy life, have fun, and be prosperous as you grow into the fullest expression of you. You are entitled to the spiritual, intellectual, and emotional freedom that you were intended to have.

Our book seeks to increase your awareness of yourself as a creative being born with potential for success, no matter what your background or experiences. You have a right to the life you desire. We have all felt trapped in our lives and lost hope of changing our circumstances at one time or another. To continue to feel trapped, however, is only because we believe in our limitations and we don't know how to change. Whatever your beliefs, we would like to point out that there is no downside to believing in something greater than

Introduction

yourself. You could spend much time arguing against the idea of Infinite Intelligence or trying to prove it, or you could relax and entertain the possibility for a while.

According to author and philosopher Charles Haanel, having a spiritual connection paves the way and opens many door:

> Spirit, whatever else it may or may not be, must be considered as the essence of consciousness, the substance of mind, the reality underlying thought. And as all ideas are phases of the activity of consciousness, mind or thought, it follows that in Spirit, and in it alone, is to be found the ultimate fact, the real thing, or idea.

All the great thinkers have admitted that man is more than his physical body, that he also is a soul, connected to divine consciousness. Emerson expressed this when he said:

> What we commonly call man, the eating, drinking, planting, counting man, does not, as we know him, represent himself, but misrepresents himself. Him we do not respect, but the soul, whose organ he is, would he let it appear through his action, would make our knees bend. When it breathes through his intellect, it is genius; when it breathes through his will, it is virtue; when it flows through his affection, it is love.

This book is the compilation of the wisdom of six different authors, all connected through a mastermind to a vision of freedom. It is a practical guide for you to follow so you can experience your own sense of possibility and the easing of fear and anxiety. We would like you to claim your dreams and learn that thought followed by progressive action will inevitably create and give physical form to that thought. We continue learning how to do this, and we welcome you to your own journey of expansion of your self, and the claiming of your birthright — freedom and joy.

With love and endless gratitude to you, we introduce you to your *7 Keys to Freedom*.

Chapter 1

The Mind

Freedom to take 100% responsibility for your life.

By Selwa Hamati

"Your mind is the greatest power in all creation."

~ Dr. J.B. Rhine

I was recently asked to speak at a women's brunch. When I walked into the room, I found beautifully decorated tables and dolls everywhere. The theme was "Childhood Memories." As announcements and acknowledgments were being made, one of the women (let's call her Dee) told us this amazing, true story about an encounter between Dee's dolls, another woman, and several city and county staff and volunteers. Here's the gist of what happened:

Dee was planning her daughter's baby shower. She had put two of her beautiful, extraordinarily lifelike dolls on a blanket in the backseat of her car. Also on the backseat was her daughter's wedding album. There was a special conference on Saturday that Dee planned to attend, after which she would go to her daughter's house to spend time with her and prepare for the baby shower.

Street parking was not available, so Dee parked in a garage nearby and walked over to where the conference was being held. At some point during the day, a woman parked next to Dee's car. When she stepped out of the car, she happened to glance into the backseat of Dee's car where she saw two "babies" wrapped in a blanket. The woman panicked and ran over to the attendant to have him call 911. She told him that there were two babies abandoned in the backseat of a car in his garage!

The attendant called 911 and then followed the woman to the car where the babies were sleeping. As they were trying to figure out a way to get into the car and rescue these poor babies, they noticed the wedding album lying next to them. Their imaginations ran wild. They thought for sure that the mom had left her two babies to die in the car while she ran off somewhere to kill herself. The woman who found these babies was now hysterical, and the attendant was trying to calm her down while figuring out a way to get into the car.

Soon the fire truck arrived. The firefighters tried to unlock the car door but could not, so they broke a window to get in there and rescue these poor babies. When they got in, they felt for the babies' pulse. Nothing ... it was too late. Everyone thought the babies were dead! The woman who found them was now hyperventilating and out of control. By now the medics had arrived. They had to take care of this woman, who had now passed out, as well as see what they could do for the little babies. Unfortunately, they, too, could not feel a pulse, and as a last resort one of them decided to look into the babies' eyes for any sign of life. That is when the medic discovered that the "babies" were actually dolls.

Wow! I couldn't believe that this had really happened. Everyone was laughing when Dee told the story, but when you stop to really think about it, it's not at all funny; it's actually quite sad. How often do we build a nightmare for ourselves based on nothing more than the appearance of things? How often do we arrive at conclusions based on nothing more than a mere glance at the facts?

The poor woman in that parking garage jumped to the worst conclusion. She assumed that a distraught mom had abandoned her two babies and taken her own life. See how easily and quickly she was able to build the nightmare? What is even scarier is how contagious nightmares can be. One person's panic causes another person to panic and the domino effect begins; from bad to worse it goes, and it picks up speed along the way.

Although people think that perception is reality, it is not. Perception creates your reality — your reality, based on what you have assumed and believed. I like this quote by Dennis Deaton: "The eye sees what the mind looks for." Our minds are powerful, and we need to know how to effectively use them.

I am not a psychotherapist, but I have read and heard about the formula that is taught them: $A + B = C$.

The Mind

    A   What happens to you in life.
 + B   Your interpretation of what happens to you in life.
    C   How you act.

So our interpretation of what happens to us in life is really our truth, because our actions are based on our interpretations–our perceptions.

Dr. Daniel Amen, a brain imaging specialist, refers to ANTs (automatic negative thoughts). Based on the story of the two dolls, can you see how ANT infestations can take over your mind and cause you to do things that you wouldn't ordinarily do? We must take care not to let these infestations happen to begin with, but when they do happen, we must be aware of the situation and be prepared to do something about it, like kill those ANTs before the infestation gets out of control.

Why is it that when things go well and you feel super happy, you tend to stop yourself from enjoying the situation too much because you fear you may "get used to it" and set yourself up for disappointment? You think, "This is too good to be true. I wonder how long it's going to last." Then you begin to self-sabotage. Think about it: if you do not do this, then you must know someone who does. Too many people waste beautiful opportunities by thinking, "What if it doesn't work out?" Well, what if it *does* work out?

We are intelligent human beings, independent thinkers. The problem is that most people have gotten so used to doing things by habit that they don't think for themselves anymore. They live unconsciously. Somewhere along our journeys, we let a few "powerful" people take charge of our important decisions and eventually gave them control over more of our lives until we stopped thinking for ourselves altogether. We gave away our power to other people who "know better than we do" about us. It doesn't make sense, does it? So we must take charge of our lives again.

I realize it is important to have good leaders, but the danger lies in giving away all of our power. We think that "they" know best, are more educated, richer, more powerful, or more experienced. So we lean on "them" to take care of some of the most important things in our lives, and we get involved in busywork. We think that when we busily run around, taking care of everything and everybody but ourselves, then we are doing what is right, what is expected of us or our "duty." Well, "busyness" has nothing to do with taking care of real business.

What happens, in most cases, when we hand over all of our decision making to someone else? We think of ourselves as victims; we feel helpless, and then we begin to blame other people for our problems. We give away our responsibilities because it's easier for someone else to get the job done, and then we blame that someone for our plight when things don't work out the way we want them to. Who is better equipped to take care of my business than me? I can seek help, but I must be the one to determine the kind of help I want.

So we must wake up from our hypnotic state and take one hundred percent responsibility for our lives, actions, and well-being. It may seem harder in the beginning, but it sure beats having someone else take charge of my life! As personal development leader Jim Rohn said, we must make a choice between experiencing the pain of discipline or the pain of regret. Which pain will you choose?

I would like to introduce you to some brilliant information about the mind that can help you take charge of your life. This information has changed my life. Please receive it with an open mind and take the time to apply it.

When we think, we mostly think in pictures. If I say "house," a picture of a house pops up on the screen of your mind; if I say "car," you see a picture of a car, and so on. Now, if I say, "mind," what picture pops into your mind? There is usually confusion about this one. Did you, perhaps, see a picture of a brain? Many people do. I did, until the difference between the brain and the mind was explained to me. People become confused because they don't know what the mind looks like.

The mind is the invisible part of your personality, so it's no wonder you don't know what it looks like. Since we live in an orderly universe, and as highly intelligent beings functioning in an orderly, intelligent manner, we do not like being in a state of confusion. Therefore, we need an image or picture of the mind to create order.

In the early 1900s, Dr. Thurman Fleet noticed this dilemma and decided to do something about it. He recognized that the mind is the invisible part of our personalities, and since he believed in treating the whole person by getting to the root of a problem (the cause), rather than simply treating symptoms, he came up with this remarkable graphic–what we call "The Stickperson."

The Mind

The Stickperson

At first glance, it may seem the picture is upside down, but this is done on purpose. You see, until now, we have given all of our conscious awareness and attention to our physical body and our five physical senses, when everything in our life is nothing but an expression of our mind, where our thinking begins and where our intellectual faculties reside. Our mind initiates and creates our actions.

Now that you have a picture of the mind, you can better understand how it works. The mind is divided into two parts: conscious (thinking) mind and subconscious (feeling) mind.

The Stickperson

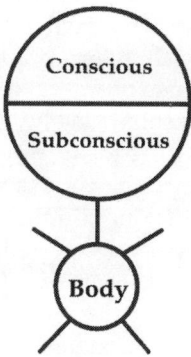

When we combine our thoughts with our feelings, they produce action (through our bodies), and our actions then produce results. This is very similar to the psychotherapist formula mentioned earlier: A + B = C.

When you think positive, happy thoughts you feel good, and your actions reflect those positive thoughts. When you think negative thoughts, you feel bad, and your actions reflect those negative thoughts. It sounds simple, I know — and it is simple, yet so misunderstood. This is the Law of Attraction in action, and it is the foundation of everything we do in life, so I believe it is very important. We must pay attention to this "simple stuff," understand how it works, and then take action and apply it in our lives.

The conscious mind has the ability to accept or reject any introduced thought. The problem is that the majority of us do not use this ability; we allow all kinds of garbage to enter our minds without ever stopping it. The subconscious mind, on the other hand, cannot reject anything; it must accept whatever you put into it. Think of your mind as a radio or television. Whatever channel you tune into creates the broadcast you receive.

Remember what I said about giving your power away somewhere along your journey? Well, here is how you can claim it back: the subconscious mind is where all of your "paradigms" reside, such as your current beliefs, your memories, and your self-image. So if we are not careful about what thoughts we allow into our conscious mind, our subconscious mind will accept whatever thoughts we feed it. It has no control over what to believe and what not to believe; it just takes it all in. Our thoughts are then mixed with our feelings, and together they produce actions, which in turn produce our results.

A good way to examine your mind is to take a good, honest look at your results, because results don't lie. You see them all around you in your environment; they are the mirror of your mind. If you do not like your results, go back to the very root of the problem and take a look at what is going on in your mind. Once you fix that, your results will change. This is how it works, period. Author James Allen said it well: "We think in secret and it comes to pass, environment is but our looking glass."

So, what influences your thoughts, and how can you control what you think about?

The Mind

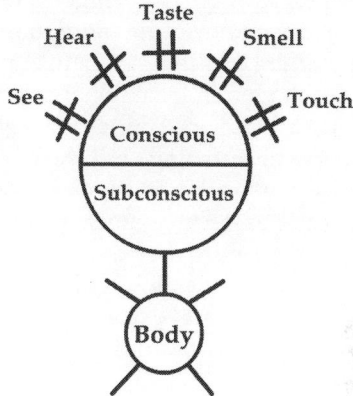

You have five physical senses; you see, hear, smell, taste, and touch. We are conditioned to learn through these senses from a very young age. It is as though our senses are hardwired to our conscious mind like little antennas, so this is how we gather most of our information from the world around us. We must be aware that these senses are always on. When you get up in the morning and open your eyes, you immediately see; you don't have to think about telling your eyes to start seeing. The same goes for smelling, hearing, and so on.

Since these senses are always on, they are constantly being bombarded by our environment through television, radio, computers, and the people around us. We have been so conditioned to live through these senses that we go about our daily living in an unconscious state — we do things in a certain way, out of habit. We are also worried about what people think and about "looking good" in front of them. Strong conditioning and tuning into our outside world keeps us on an emotional roller coaster for most of our lives. When someone pays us a compliment, we feel good; a few minutes later someone criticizes us, and we immediately feel bad. One minute we are up; the next moment we are going down fast.

So if you want to change this madness and improve your results, you must be aware of who and what you listen to. You must guard your thoughts (conscious mind) as though your life depends on them — because it does. Once you become aware of how the mind works and understand the process, then you can go to work on the inside to change your outside environment (your physical results).

Now let me warn you that, as intelligent human beings created for a specific purpose, we know a lot more than we realize. But did you know that the biggest gap in life is between what we know and what we actually do? I'm reminded of what psychotherapist Nathaniel Branden said: "We are the one species that can formulate a vision of what values are worth pursuing, and then pursue the opposite." Why? Why do we not pursue those visions and values that are worth pursuing? Because it is easier to remain stuck in our old ways of thinking and doing what we are used to doing. We experience strong resistance in the form of huge, self-created barriers when we attempt to change. This feeling can prevent us from taking the necessary steps to achieve the results we want. We get scared or anxious, and ask ourselves questions like, "What will people say if I don't do this, or if I do that?" Rather than pursuing what we value, we wind up settling for the familiar and staying in what we call our "comfort zone."

Keep this in mind as you face your challenges: growth requires getting uncomfortable. "Good" is not always good enough. As a matter of fact, "good" is the enemy of "best." It is each individual's duty to step up and live their best life possible, as they define it for themselves. No excuses!

It is crucial to understand that your current results do not reflect your potential. Your current results are a direct by-product of your previous thinking — the way you thought until this moment. Previous thinking may have limited you in the past, but you are by no means trapped by it. You have infinite potential, limited only by your own thoughts. So, if you want to change your results, you must first change your thoughts. You do have choices — even in matters out of your control, you have choices. It's all in the way you look at things, your own interpretation of what happens to you in life.

We tend to look to others (family, friends and associates) for advice when we pursue what we want in life. If you follow this strategy, the question you must ask yourself is this: Is the person you are looking to for advice qualified to give it? If you want to learn how to swim, you must find someone who knows how to swim well and is willing and able to teach you. You would not go to someone who knows nothing about swimming and has never been in the water, would you?

Now, let's consider better ways to influence our thoughts independent of our environment. You will want to learn how to use your mind with a higher intensity by engaging, enabling, and using it to think with your own intellect and thoughts. In doing so, you will not need to rely on others to make your own choices. You see, we all know our five physical senses, but few people know what intellectual faculties are. You have six intellectual faculties. The directed use of these faculties allows you to control the way you think, and since they are like mental muscles, you can develop and strengthen them through exercise — mental exercise. When these faculties are developed and used properly, you can enhance your thoughts and produce whatever results you want in your life.

Our intellectual faculties are these: imagination, memory, reason, perception, intuition, and will. Let's take a brief look at each one.

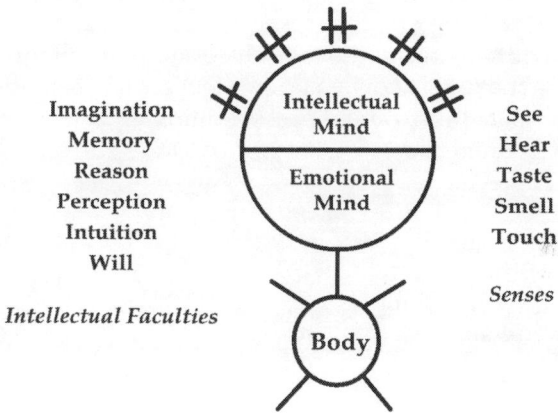

Imagination

Your imagination is your ability to build big, beautiful pictures in your mind. It is the workshop of the mind. We can use our imaginations to build nightmares or beautiful dreams. Most of us have not used our imaginations properly since we were small children. Remember when you could take a box, especially a big appliance box, and turn it into a fort or playhouse? How about a blanket and a couple of chairs? They made for a cool tent! But then we had to "grow up" and go off to school, where there was not much time to dream like we once did. Slowly but surely, we stopped using our imaginations properly and learned to follow instructions and do what we were told to do.

Having these things brought to your awareness, you can now use your imagination to build big, beautiful pictures of all the things you do want in your life, instead of continuing to focus on the things you don't want, and building the nightmares that go with them.

Memory

We are not concerned about whether you have a good memory or not; it's the content of your memory that counts. You were born with an awareness of your success, but you may remember and dwell on your failures instead of your successes. Is your mind filled with empowering, life-affirming memories that excite and pull you forward? If not, then this book will show you how to use your memory as a tool to be free from faulty logic and past conditioning so that you can experience the freedom to create whatever you want with your life.

Reason

Reason gives you the ability to think, choose, and make decisions. It is the highest function that you, as an intelligent being, are capable of. You can use your reason to succeed in life, rather than to argue for your limitations.

Instead of gathering information from your senses, nature's lower side, you will want to develop and use your higher side — your intellect. This is really what separates us from animals. When we use our higher/intellectual side, we begin to change the way we look at things and take control of our lives. Like the skipper of a sailboat, you cannot help where the wind blows, but you sure can set the sail. This is how you ultimately change your results.

Perception

This is how you see your world. It's your point of view. Your perception is how you accept the world and at the same time your projection of the world. Your eyes see what your mind directs them to see, and this, therefore, is what you receive. Is your cup half full or half empty? The Law of Polarity, one of the natural laws of the universe, states that everything has a polar opposite. With every up, there is a corresponding down; with every in, there is an out; and with every front, there is a back. So we must choose to see the good in everything. Dr. Wayne Dyer said it best: "When we change the way we look at things, the things we look at change." I remember the day I chose to change the way I looked at things as though it were yesterday. I hadn't even heard of Dr. Dyer at that point, but when I saw and heard this quote, I knew exactly what he meant. This is nothing short of total transformation!

Decide today to accept what is. You have no control over others or the environment as a whole; you can only control yourself and the choices you make. So don't waste your energy trying to change what you have no control over; use it to make yourself a better person. Choose wisely. Remember the Serenity Prayer?

"God grant me the serenity to accept the things I cannot change, courage to change the things I can, and wisdom to know the difference."

Intuition

This is your ability to pick up energy that is all around you. Some people call it a sixth sense, coincidence, hunch, or gut feeling. Have you ever been in a room full of people, when someone walks in and you just get a bad "vibe" from that person? If you are tuned in to your intuition, you will know there is something not quite right; you feel the negative energy from that person. Your intuition is designed to show you the opportunities in your life to move you forward and guide you toward your goal.

I like the way Wayne Dyer describes intuition: "Prayer is when we talk to God; intuition is when God talks to us."

Will

Will is the ability to concentrate and stay focused on an idea to the exclusion of all others and to willingly take action in alignment with that idea. Emerson said, "The only thing that can grow is the thing we give energy to." You have to have an unwavering certainty that you will achieve your goals. If you allow circumstances to easily distract you, you will not be successful.

If you want specific desired results, then you must use your will to help hold your beautiful pictures on the screen of your mind and be willing to take action aligned with your desired results.

Do you see how these amazing faculties work together so naturally?

You are a spiritual being, living in a physical body, gifted with a magnificent intellect. So rather than living by old paradigms (conditioning), and always thinking from the outside in, tune in to your internal channel and begin living from the inside out.

Use your intellectual faculties, get excited about them, and let them guide you on your journey from where you are to where you want to go. Your mind is one of the most powerful engines of success. Develop it, use it properly, and take charge of your own life!

We are now living in the information age, and there is no reason why any of us should live a less than abundant and fulfilled life. If you don't believe me, find out for yourself — do some research, study successful people, explore the possibilities. At the end of the day, however, you must take action. When you do, you will attract massive abundance and live the life of your dreams!

It is imperative as you review and/or set your goals, that you make sure these goals are your own. You will feel frustrated living someone else's expectations — and that seldom leads to real success, if ever.

Here's the absolute bottom line: if you really want different results, you must do things differently. You must think differently. Positive change on all levels, including material success, begins on the inside. So spend a few minutes every day reflecting and examining your thought process to understand the cause of your actions, and moving forward, change or enhance your results.

"The opposite of courage in our society is not cowardice, it is conformity." - Dr. Rollo May

Selwa Hamati, USA

Chapter 2

Your Imagination

The key to dreaming BIG and Beautifully.

By Gwen Boudreau

"Life isn't about finding yourself, it's about creating yourself."

~ George Bernard Shaw

The first time I came across that quote by George Bernard Shaw, a light bulb went on in my head. I had wasted so much of my life trying to figure out who I was, hoping it would be shown to me through my higher power, friends, family, colleagues, and educators, or through my travels. I finally realized that the entire time, it was really up to me who I wanted to be! It was a life-changing moment and such an amazing concept. I had always envisioned myself as a loving wife and mother, a woman who connects well with others, as a creative individual and so much more, but I was waiting for someone else to tell me that I was all of these things instead of believing myself that I was.

Truth be told, when someone did tell me I was any of these things, I would not believe them anyway because of my low self-image. I was often envious of other people's gifts and talents, wishing I could be more like them or have what they had. Instead of realizing and focusing on my own strengths, I focused on other people's strengths and believed I was not as good as they were. I had the mindset that other people, perhaps more deserving people, possessed these qualities and that I would never have them. I believed that other people could accomplish the goals that I had dreamed of my whole life, yet I felt that I could not achieve them. In 2006, the year *The Secret* came out, I was finally becoming aware that it was my responsibility to create my life. I was finally beginning to take one-hundred-percent responsibility for my own thoughts and the results I was getting in my life.

The most intriguing part of all of this is that throughout my entire life — from the time I was a little girl — I felt deep in my heart that I was gifted and special. I always stood out, whether it was for my sweet smile and demeanor as a young girl, my contagious enthusiasm and zest for life, or my compassion and desire to help others. I have always felt this greatness inside of me, and yet I was consistently self-sabotaging and getting in the way of my gifts by focusing on my weaknesses. Do you know that greatness lies within you? Have you ever felt it? I hope so for your sake and for the sake of our beautiful world, because your gifts are as unique and as special as you are, and they will provide tremendous service to our world if you use them.

So here I was, at the age of 36, with a poor self-image on one hand, yet feeling a sense of greatness deep within me on the other hand. Talk about a contradiction! My entire life, I wanted to make my mark and contribution to the world. I would always imagine myself being interviewed, winning a prestigious award, giving a speech, or meeting a public figure that I admired and imagining our wonderful conversations. Why was it always these scenarios playing over in my mind?

One of the gifts I have been blessed with is my beautiful imagination. Since I was a child, I have always had an amazing imagination, and I was always in a state of wonder. I was a 13-year-old who still believed in Santa Claus! I will never forget the night my father and sister told me that there was no such thing as Santa. It was on Christmas Eve, and my mother was fighting for her life in the hospital. I was heartbroken. Not only could I lose my mother any day, but now there was no Santa Claus. As I look back on the situation, I realize that at some point I would have to learn that Santa Claus was a historical, imaginary figure. My younger sister already knew that there was no Santa Claus, but I would not believe her. I was asking Santa to make my mommy healthy so she could come home to us, and all of a sudden there was no Santa Claus for me to ask anymore. Who was going to grant my Christmas wish now? Who has the right to take another person's hope away?

I always heard, "Take off those rose-colored glasses," and "That's not realistic." For many years, I shut down that part of me that loved to dream. I dreamed the realistic dreams of getting married and settling down to have a family. Don't get me wrong, these were big dreams of mine as well, but I had other dreams too. So I did not always see my imagination as a gift. It seemed to be a hindrance at times and everyone thought I was a dreamer, as if it was a bad thing. I know now that it is an amazing gift.

About six years ago, the same dreams I had when I was a child kept popping into my head. How could this be? I had given up on those dreams years ago. It was my dream and vision of working in film and television. In my early 20s, I had worked briefly out in Vancouver, British Columbia on television and movie sets as a production assistant, with the vision of someday becoming an actress, writer, producer, and director. But at the age of 24, I shut the dream down, and now this voice inside of me kept creeping into my heart. I did not understand why this was happening to me. After voicing this several times and struggling to find my way through it, all I heard from those who "loved" me were comments like, "Bear with her, it's just a phase." "What about the children?" "Where is all of this coming from, Gwen?" I can tell you now that it was my intuition at work; that soft voice that is the essence of who I am was reaching out to me, because I was not following my heart's desire.

After more than a year of going through the ups and downs, the push and pull, of trying to obliterate these thoughts and push these desires further away, I found myself taking a good, long look at where I was, and doing my best with the awareness that I had to make sense of it all. Here I was at the age of 37, and I was not pursuing the career of my dreams; I was not earning the income I wanted to earn, although my husband provided a life that most people could only dream about; I was in a marriage that I had outgrown and did not want to be in anymore because my spirit was dying. Yet I had three babies under the age of three and I had been in this relationship for nine years. I kept wondering over and over, "Do I break up my family in order for me to survive? or do I stay, knowing I will be giving up a huge part of who I am so that my babies can have their family together and live with both their mommy and daddy?"

I knew what I had to do. It killed me inside to destroy one of the things I dreamed of having my whole life — my family! I had to stand up for my true self, the person I was at the time, and the woman I knew I could become. I wanted to be a role model for my children and to show them that life is nothing without following your passion and taking chances. I wanted to be a role model for other women in similar situations as my own. I wanted to take my personal power back and prove to myself that I could l do this and live the life that I always dreamed of living.

It is my intent to guide you throughout this chapter, on the intellectual faculty of imagination. I want to provide you with an understanding of what imagination is; to help you reconnect with your imagination, and to develop your imagination to create abundance, joy, ease and balance in all areas of your life. Most importantly to help you understand that everything that occurs on the outside is first originated on the inside. You can unlock your success DNA by using these *7 Keys to Freedom* through understanding how change is created in our mind, having a clear picture of the mind and how the mind works, and learning more about each of the six intellectual faculties and developing them.

Imagination and Your Paradigms

From reading the chapter on The Mind, you know how your marvelous mind works. Remember, the mind is the invisible part of your personality, and to understand the mind you must first have an image to work from. Go back for a moment to the chapter and review the Stickperson diagram. The mind is divided into two parts: the conscious and the subconscious mind. The conscious mind is hooked up to our five senses through sight, sound, taste, touch, and smell. Our senses are like little antennae that are picking up all the information from the outside world. You hear it and smell it; it's coming in through taste and touch, and you see images on television and in print. This information bombards your conscious mind through both positive and negative messages and images. The conscious mind is also the intellectual mind and the intellectual mind holds your intellectual faculties, which are imagination, memory, reason, perception, intuition, and will. These are the faculties that cause your paradigms to change. Your paradigms are your habits and attitudes that cause you to think, feel, and act toward yourself and others as you do. They were built without your permission and before you had the ability to think for yourself. When you were born, you hadn't yet established your thinking mind. Your mind was filled, over the years, with thoughts and habits of those who loved you and those who were responsible for you, such as your parents, grandparents, caregivers, teachers and other authority figures. Your mind was filled with their images and ideas of who they thought you should become. So essentially they built your self-image. Since we have been programmed from infancy to rely on our physical senses and outside influences to interpret the world we live in, the question becomes, How do you start to create your new self-image? We will come back to this later on in the chapter.

Do you remember how vivid your imagination was when you were a child? You could play with a box for hours despite all the toys you had around you. It always amazes me to see what my children can do with a cardboard box of any size. They color it and cover it with stickers; they sit in it or make it into a house, boat, or bed for their action figures and dolls. They get so much joy and laughter out of using their imaginations.

As children, we were in touch with our imaginations, yet as we grew up we were encouraged to stop dreaming and to conform to the masses and become "realistic." So the majority of us did just that! We stopped using our imaginations and only dreamed the socially acceptable dreams of getting married, having children, finding a secure job, and our dreams of becoming a great architect or legendary musician slowly deteriorated. Has that ever happened to you? It happened to me and the day I read, "Life isn't about finding yourself, it's about creating yourself" by George Bernard Shaw, it felt like I had been given my life back, and I claimed it immediately! The quote literally gave me permission to dream again, and this time to dream bigger than ever! That is what I want for you more than anything else. I want to ignite the passion that I know is deep within you and for you to create a life that you absolutely love.

We use imagination to create everything in our lives, both good and bad. I manifested my divorce, divided up everything we had, from homes to cutlery, and created a parenting plan the two of us would never be happy with, but could live with. I had challenges and stumbling blocks to work through. I had many sleepless nights trying to create my new place in this world. There were many days I wanted to give up, and crawl into a hole and die. Most days, however, I did what I had to do because I knew in my heart that I was creating a better life for me and ultimately for my children. I recreated my entire life over the next five years. I reclaimed my spirit and my sense of wonder about our beautiful world. I learned to surround myself with people who want to see me grow and succeed in every aspect of it. I also removed people from my life because they sucked the energy out of me with their negative thoughts and views. I realized that as I grew personally, everything in my life grew in proportion.

I started Punch Bowl Productions in 2008 with no idea of what I was doing, but I knew that if I wanted to follow my passion and create relevant television, then I needed to take inspired action — and this was the first step. I put myself out there as often as I could to meet and network with people in the industry and to build and nurture those relationships. I can now confidently walk into any event and speak with anyone about who I am and what my vision is for my company and myself. Today, I couldn't be happier. I am following my heart's desire and my passion, which is being a loving and dedicated mother, and a writer. I am creating and developing programs with my colleagues, and helping others identify their dreams and achieve their goals. The more "unreasonable" the goal, the better I like it!

You can create the life of your dreams! Have you ever heard of anything so amazing? You can be, do, and have anything you want. Napoleon Hill said, "You will never have a definite purpose in life; you will never have self-confidence; you will never have initiative and leadership, unless you first create these qualities in your imagination and see yourself in possession of them." Hill was an American author considered to be one of the great writers and first producers of personal success literature, and he wrote the best-selling book, *Think and Grow Rich* (1937). He studied and analyzed more than 500 exceedingly wealthy men over a period of 25 years and then wrote his book, which outlines the proven steps to riches through thoughts, ideas and organized plans. It all starts by changing our minds from failure consciousness to success consciousness. In other words, once you move from a poverty mindset to a prosperity mindset, your dominating thoughts of prosperity will attract the forces, people and circumstances that harmonize with those dominating thoughts in your mind. This is The Law of Attraction at work. The key is that it all begins in the imagination. You must create the qualities you seek in your imagination and perceive yourself already in possession of them.

What is Imagination?

Imagination is the intellectual faculty out of which visions arise. Imagination is the creative workshop of the mind. The one thing that all great leaders of the world have taught us is that we become what we think about. Each one was at first a natural dreamer. Columbus imagined a new world and discovered it; Copernicus imagined there was a multiplicity of worlds and revealed them; Albert Einstein imagined the expansion of Newtonian mechanics and thus developed the theory of relativity; the Wright Brothers imagined us being propelled through the air; Dr. Alexander Graham Bell imagined a way to transmit speech; Thomas Edison imagined electric-power generation and distribution to homes, businesses and factories; Henry Ford imagined an automobile that was affordable to all of middle-class America; and Dr. Wernher von Braun imagined a booster rocket to help land the first man on the moon.

Hill said, "The great leaders of business, industry, finance, and the great artists, musicians, poets, and writers became great, because they developed the faculty of creative imagination." This is the part of our higher self where inspirations and ideas are received. Hill goes on to say that:

> The imagination is literally the workshop wherein are fashioned all plans created by man. The impulse, the DESIRE, is given shape, form, and ACTION through the aid of the imaginative faculty of the mind. It has been said that man can create anything which he can imagine.

Our whole world revolves around images. If I ask you to think of a car, what is the first thing you see? Is it the word "car" flashing before your eyes? Probably not. I would expect it to be an image of a car. Perhaps even an image of your car, or your dream car. If I ask you to think of a rainbow, do you envision a rainbow? Do you see a beautiful, full rainbow with all seven colors in it — red, orange, yellow, green, blue, indigo and violet? If I ask you to recall a memory such as what you wore on your wedding day or your favorite vacation, you would describe it to me as you envision it happening on the screen of your mind. Imagination is the work of the mind that helps create and build big, beautiful pictures. No one has any more imagination than anyone else. It is how you use your imagination that makes the difference. You use your imagination every day when you pick out clothes to wear, plan a vacation or a party, even when you give directions or describe an event. If this is the only time you use your imagination, then your imaginative faculty may be weak from inactivity. However, a highly developed imagination strengthens your creative abilities. It is a great tool for recreating and transforming your life. A highly developed imagination becomes strengthened and more alert with use.

Self-Image and Your Imagination

Every individual possesses his or her own self-image. Your self-image is your own idea of who you are. Remember, I mentioned earlier that those who were responsible for you in your younger years helped to build your self-image. Your experiences, successes and failures also contribute to the building of your self-image. Your self-image imposes limits on your beliefs about your personal value and abilities. The self-image that you hold is like a cybernetic mechanism: it is set on a certain level of acceptance of your capabilities, and the moment you go off-course, the mechanism activates to set you back on course. We could compare it to the automatic pilot of an airplane: the moment it goes off-course, the cybernetic mechanism or communication controls in the airplane readjust and set the plane back on course. If you believe yourself to be a successful individual, then any failure will be seen by your cybernetic mechanism as "going off-course" and you very soon will be back on track to your "successful" self. If you hold a poor self-image of yourself, then any success or breakthrough you experience will be accepted as "going off-course" and your cybernetic mechanism will soon set you back on track to live as you have been trained to do with limiting beliefs and fears.

"Your success in any undertaking will never be greater than the image you have of yourself." ~ Bob Proctor

To be worth more, you have to be worthy of more. Any person can alter their self-image, and by doing so, they take full responsibility for their life and control over their situations and circumstances.

Working with your self-image is a process of awareness, choices, focus and dedication. Your goals and desires are the seeds to discover your real purpose and to help you grow in your awareness of who you are and the person you want to become. Remember what the great George Bernard Shaw said: "Life is not about finding yourself, it is about creating yourself."

One of the greatest discoveries in modern psychology was made in the 1960s by the plastic surgeon Dr. Maxwell Maltz in his revolutionary book *Psycho-Cybernetics*. Dr. Maltz believed that a person's self-image was the cornerstone of their success. He felt people should have a positive view of themselves or else all of their efforts will end in defeat, and they will continue to be stuck in their paradigms or limiting beliefs. He was giving his patients a good image on the outside, yet he noticed that sometimes, even when the operation was successful, that the patient was no happier. This was because of their poor self-image, therefore, no amount of surgery to change their outer appearance would help them find happiness if there is no positive self-image within.

The self-image is what you perceive yourself to be on a deep subconscious level. Most people are not aware of this self-image because nature has hidden it in our subconscious or unconscious minds. Your self-image determines who you are and what you are capable of doing. You are never too old or too young to work on your self-image. I recently bought a canvas with the word "Believe" on it and when my six-year-old daughter saw it for the first time, she asked me what it said so I told her. Her response was, "Believe in yourself." I was speechless when she said it. We hope as parents that what we teach our children is sinking in, and I was overjoyed when she said that! The pride I felt in her and in myself at that very moment is indescribable. The idea is to form a positive self-image that you hold of yourself, and plug it into your subconscious mind. As your mind remembers your natural perfection, you will become a master of your life. All your achievements, desires, and wants will be in harmony with your self-image.

Your self-image determines who you are and what you are capable of doing. All your actions, feelings, and behaviors are always consistent with your self-image. Within the faculty of imagination, self-image is about creating your new positive self. Use your imagination to build the picture of yourself; use your perception to see yourself as worthy; use your reasoning to choose if it is good for you; use your will to help you stay focused; and use your memory to imprint it in your mind. Your intuition will guide you in this effort as you build your self-image. Let your heart's desire be your guide. It is about you and your ability to allow yourself to be the person you have always wanted to be.

The Creative Process

> "Imagination is the beginning of creation. You imagine what you desire, you will what you imagine and at last you create what you will." ~ George Bernard Shaw

Let's think about this idea of "creating your own life" for a moment. What exactly does that mean? How do you create the life of your dreams? A series of steps that make up the creative process will help turn your desires into reality. Remember that everything around you was once just a thought, an idea conceived in the imagination.

Fantasy is the first stage of creation in life. It is created in your conscious mind through your imagination. The function of the imagination is creating a vision, and the function of the vision is in the details. As you begin this process, imagine you are watching a movie, and you are the star! I want you to get very clear about what you want. Write it out in great detail and be very specific. What do you see? What are you wearing? What are you doing? Who are you with? Where are you? How do you feel? I want you to be associated with your vision, meaning that I want you to see this vision through your own eyes as opposed to just watching yourself in the movie. The more specific you can be, the easier it is to invoke emotions within you, and when our thoughts are combined with feelings they produce actions (through our body), and our actions produce our results. The goal is to eventually think about your fantasy and to immediately have that equivocal feeling or emotion that you have attached to the fantasy vibrate throughout your entire body, which allows you to vibrate on a new level or frequency.

Most people are unaware that they have a vibrational frequency. The Law of Vibration and Attraction, which manages the universe and everything that exists, is a law that responds to vibrational frequencies. Everything vibrates; nothing rests. Conscious awareness of vibration is called feeling. Your thoughts control your vibration (feeling), which dictates what you attract. When that vibration of desire is truly active within you, you will begin to attract those people, circumstances, and things that you need to turn your fantasy into reality.

The second step in the creative process is theory. The word "theory" comes from the Greek word *"theoria"* meaning contemplation. If you want to change your current results, you must begin to think differently. So, turning fantasy into theory requires a shift in attitude. William James said, "The greatest discovery of my generation is that a human being can alter his life by altering his attitudes of mind." Attitude is the vibration you are in right now, which is determined by the thoughts you choose to get emotionally involved with. Attitude is expressed through your actions. A negative attitude will move you into a bad vibration whereas a positive attitude will instantly move you into a positive vibration. You will find this shift in attitude occur as you exercise your intellectual faculties. The moment you become emotionally involved with the image you give form to the fantasy.

I am sure that this material is stretching you into some different ways of looking at things. Normally, our first reaction when we are being challenged or contemplating something is to go straight back to what we have been trained to do, which is to go back to our old paradigms and habits and continue to react to the outside world because it seems easier. I want to applaud you for working your way through all of these new ideas to expand your mind for the betterment of yourself and your life. I want you to know that you have a power within you that is far superior to any condition or situation presently around you. Holding these thoughts and desires with your will, which is the faculty by which a person decides on and initiates action, is the only way to break through your old paradigms and turn your fantasy into theory.

The third and final step in the creative process is fact. You must be willing to do whatever is required to turn theory into a whole new set of positive facts. The minute you launch a desire into the world, it is already complete and being held for you. All you have to do is be willing to do the work required to achieve your desires. Willingness is your will in action. If you want to be healthier there is more work for you to do, not only in terms of choosing to eat a healthier, more balanced diet and moving your body, but also by releasing old paradigms and creating a positive self-image. If you want to be more prosperous, there is more work to be done through letting go of old conditioning and perceiving and believing yourself as worthy.

You must be focused and willing to persist long enough, and do whatever is necessary to receive the reward you desire. Your belief should be so strong that you naturally expect the reward. The moment you are willing to commit and take inspired action, the theory or goal turns into a fact and it begins to move into physical form.

There is a wonderful quote by Patricia Shambrook, who said, "Don't give me the facts, give me the truth. The facts are always changing." Imagination gives you the freedom to create yourself the way you want. We have been programmed to look at the facts: "I don't have enough money," "I am overweight," "I am stupid." But the truth lies in the reality of the image we hold in our minds. It is the complete opposite of what we have been trained to do as humans. We have lost our imaginations. We have lost that picture of ourselves as pure spirit before we were trained away from our essence. *7 Keys to Freedom* is the how-to guide to recapture who we really are. The truth is we are perfect.

> "First comes thought; then organization of that thought, into ideas and plans; then transformation of those plans into reality. The beginning, as you will observe, is in your imagination." ~ Napoleon Hill

Understanding Imagination

The creative process begins with your imagination and ends with the requirement and commitment from you to take inspired action and do whatever is necessary to achieve your goals and receive the reward you seek. To further understand the imaginative faculty, there are some important ideas to examine to help you achieve the wonderful life you are seeking. These ideas are abstract, meaning existing in thought, but they do not have a physical or concrete existence. They include responsibility, desire, belief, and persistence. Let's look at these abstract ideas to see the role they play in helping us understand imagination.

Responsibility

As you begin this transformation process of creating your life of abundance, joy, ease, and balance, you must first take a look at your results and remember that understanding precedes change. If we take a look back at the Stickperson in the chapter on The Mind, we are reminded that your present results are the mirror image of your combined thoughts and feelings. Your present results come from behavior, which is caused by your paradigms. When you change your paradigms, which are your habits, you will become more aware. The awareness you are seeking requires replacing old conditioning, which is genetic and environmental. Your conscious mind (thoughts), when combined with your subconscious mind (feelings), produces a vibration throughout your body (actions), which produces your results.

Success in anything begins with personal responsibility. This is what Val Van De Wall wrote about taking responsibility:

> When a person takes responsibility for their life and the results they are obtaining, they will cease to blame others as the cause of their results. Since you cannot change other people, blame is inappropriate. Blaming others causes a person to remain bound in a prison of their own making. When you take responsibility, blame is eliminated and you are free to grow.

Your ability to accept this regardless of circumstances is key in creating the life you desire. As an exercise, take some time now to write down the results you are getting in the following areas of your life: personal relationships, finances, occupation, health, and any others that come to mind. If the results you are getting are a match to what you want, then keep on doing it! If your results are not a match to what you want, then there is more work for you to do. Assume responsibility for your thoughts and take responsibility for your outcomes. Once you do this, you are free to create your own destiny.

Desire

Desire is the starting point of all achievement. Napoleon Hill said, "Truly, thoughts are things, and powerful things at that, when they are mixed with definiteness of purpose, persistence, and a burning desire for their translation into riches, or other material objects." Coming from the place of what we really want, what we really desire, and becoming a vibrational match with that desire is what we strive for. You want to become so emotionally involved with your desire that you will stake your life on it. That's exactly what Edwin C. Barnes did when he had the burning desire to become a business associate of Thomas Edison. But Barnes had a couple of challenges. First, he did not know Thomas Edison, and second, he did not have enough money to take a train to New Jersey. That would immediately stop most people, but it didn't stop Barnes. He was ready for a business association with Thomas Edison, and he was willing to do whatever it took to achieve it. Barnes started in the company in an entry-level position. He was hungry with desire, and little by little he moved toward his goal, and his goal moved toward him. Edison invented a dictating machine that none of his sales representatives wanted to sell. Barnes, realizing that this was his opportunity, convinced Edison that he could sell the machine for him. He sold it so successfully that Edison gave him national exclusivity to distribute and market the machine, and the slogan, "Made by Edison and installed by Barnes" was born. Hill concludes:

> Barnes literally thought himself into a partnership with the great Edison! He thought himself into a fortune. He had nothing to start with, except the capacity to know what he wanted, and the determination to stand by that desire until he realized it.

Most often your clearest desires are born out of your awareness of what you don't want. The problem with this is "what you do not want" is still in the mix. Your desire is muted with worry and doubt and these contradictory thoughts create a confused vibration within you. When you predominantly think, speak, act, and focus on the things you do not want, you are calling that into existence. Listen to your thoughts. Think of the things you desire and focus intently on them. By holding the image on the screen of your mind, the people, things and circumstances you require will move toward you, and you will move toward them because it is the Law of Attraction. Your emotions are the key to your alignment or resistance to the vibration you are in.

Belief

After taking responsibility for your present thoughts and results, and after visualizing your heart's desire, the next idea you need to clearly grasp is belief. Belief is a state of expectancy. You must expect that you are going to receive what you are asking for. When you order a pizza, you expect to receive it. You do not doubt whether you have ordered it; you know you have. When you buy a new home, you do not worry that someone else is going to buy it. Even though you are not living there, you know that on the closing date you will be handed the keys to move in. There is an expectancy that takes place in those situations. You automatically know that these things are going to happen. So when you build those big, beautiful pictures in your mind of your deepest desire and launch it into the world, you must not only believe that they will manifest for you, you must know and expect that they will manifest in their physical form.

Eleanor Roosevelt said, "The future belongs to those who believe in the beauty of their dreams." Believe that you already have what you desire. Believe that the picture you have painted on the screen of your mind is already yours. If you have difficulty getting yourself to a point of believing, then make believe as a child would. Act as if you already have it. Your subconscious mind cannot tell the difference between what is real and what is imagined. Play a mental game with yourself and see yourself already in possession of your dream job, your ideal weight, your financial abundance, or whatever it is you desire. Again, the goal here is to get emotionally involved so that you become a vibrational match with your vision, and you will ultimately be able to cause the idea to manifest itself in your life. What you believe and what you expect are manifesting all around you as evidence of what you believe and what you expect.

"Believe you can and you're halfway there." ~ Theodore Roosevelt

Persistence

When your vision is clear and you are working toward it, there will inevitably be challenges along the way. Giving up is easy. We do it all the time. What would have happened if Columbus or Dr. Alexander Graham Bell gave up? Thomas Edison said, "Nearly every man who develops an idea works at it up to the point where it looks impossible, and then gets discouraged. That's not the place to become discouraged." Did you know that Thomas Edison failed thousands of times while trying to create the light bulb? Persistence is to continue on a course of action in spite of difficulty or opposition; it is a state of mind, a habit.

In his chapter on Persistence, Napoleon Hill wrote, "Too many people refuse to set high goals for themselves, or even neglect selecting a career because they fear the criticism of relatives and 'friends' who may say, 'Don't aim so high, people will think you are crazy.'" These are the people who blame circumstances and other people for their current results. These are the people who are reacting to the world, not responding to it. These are the people who are living through their senses, not their intellectual faculties. These are the people living from the outside in, not the inside out. Success is not the result of good luck or favorable breaks; success is the direct result of taking action even when you have hit a roadblock. Success is getting back up when you have been knocked down. Success is having the tenacity and courage to keep going.

> "Persistence is to the character of man as carbon is to steel."
> ~ Napoleon Hill

One of my clients shared a story with me about the power of her imagination. I would like to share it with you because it incorporates these ideas and demonstrates that when these ideas are used in conjunction with one another, success is the result. Here is Sarah's story:

> I had experienced times when I could visualize what I wanted and by creating a clear picture I could move toward that image and make it happen. I remember a winter in my early twenties when I wanted to learn how to Eskimo

roll my new kayak. I bought the kayak because I wanted to meet guys, and because I couldn't pick up a canoe and put it on top of my yellow Toyota Corolla. I figured that I needed to learn how to roll this thing so I wouldn't look like such a fool as I banged my way down the rocks of some class-three rapid river. So I drove 45 minutes once a week to an indoor pool at the YMCA to learn how to Eskimo roll my kayak. That's what you do when you flip over in white water rapids. The skirt you wear around your waist and the top of the kayak keeps the water out while you try to right yourself as you are streaming down the river getting banged up, the reason for the heavy plastic helmet.

I had upper body strength, yet I was unable to get the roll down in spite of trying for several weeks. I was convinced that being overweight was keeping me from being successful. There was no willpower that was going to help me do this because of the image I had in my mind of being too heavy. I did use persistence, though, to keep going to the pool. What drove me was the image in my mind of being on the river and being safer.

It was not until my young instructor assured me that I could do it if I started visualizing doing it in my mind. That gave me a glimmer of hope. I went home and started imagining myself hanging upside down in my kayak, keeping calm while I brought my paddle around to my right side next to the kayak, then snapping my hips while pushing down with the paddle. After a week of visualizing practice, I did it the first time in the water! I was amazed by how easy it was. Was that the trick? All I had to do was imagine being able to do something, and my body and brain would work together to make it happen?

Do you see how beautifully everything came together for Sarah? She took responsibility for the results she was getting; she had a burning desire to learn how to Eskimo roll her kayak; when she was visualizing, she placed herself in the picture and believed she had already accomplished the roll; and she was persistent. These are the new habits you need to cultivate in your subconscious mind. It all stems from your desire. Hill said this: "Weak desires bring weak results ...this weakness may be remedied by building a stronger fire under your desires." Success depends upon the intensity of your desire.

Mental Imagery

Research shows that when someone imagines him- or herself doing a physical movement, such as throwing a ball or Eskimo rolling a kayak, as in Sarah's case, it creates neural patterns in the brain as if the actual physical activity is being performed. This process is called mental imagery, or mental practice. It is the thinking rehearsal of a physical activity.

You may have heard of mental imagery being used to improve sports performance, such as golf or running. Athletes practice mental imagery because they want to condition their mind in such a way that the body automatically behaves the way they want it to without effort. Mental imagery is used in other kinds of performance, as well. In 2007, an article in *Time* magazine, "The Brain: How the Brain Rewires Itself," was published about Harvard neuroscientist Alvaro Pascual-Leone and his experiments using transcranial magnetic stimulation (TMS) to map motor cortex areas in the brain that change with activity. In his experiment, Pascual-Leone had two groups of volunteers learn and practice a five-finger piano exercise. The first group was instructed to play as fluidly as they could practice two hours a day for five days. The second group of volunteers was instructed to simply think about practicing the piano exercise and to play the piece of music in their head, holding their hand still while imagining how they would move their fingers. After each day of practice, the volunteers sat under the TMS machine to be tested. After testing both groups, the findings showed that the region of motor cortex that controls the piano-playing fingers expanded in the brains of the volunteers in both groups! These kinds of results establish mental imagery as a tool that can lead to mastery of a movement or activity with less physical effort.

The same holds true for highly successful people. If they visualize the success they want, eventually their bodies will automatically do whatever they must to make the image a physical reality. The outcome will not happen from doing it once for a few minutes, however; it happens from repeated practice. Visualizing an outcome you want repeatedly will build cells of recognition in your memory bank. Remember, the subconscious mind cannot distinguish between what is real and what is imagined, and therefore mental practice can be just as effective as actual practice.

Imagination and the Other Faculties

All the intellectual faculties work very closely with one another. As you develop and use them together, you will become more creative and more powerful, and you will get better results, ultimately creating a life of freedom — freedom from judgment, freedom from doubt, and freedom from fear.

Perception and imagination are both faculties of vision. You may imagine yourself rich and beautiful, but you must have a strong, positive self-image of yourself to be able to see yourself as such. We use our imagination to change the way something is perceived. So, create the qualities you seek in your imagination, and perceive yourself already in possession of them.

Reason without imagination leads to a weakened vision. Reason gives you the ability to think the way you want to think about any idea. Imagination helps you build big, beautiful pictures on the screen of your mind. Creating a vision using both your reason and your imagination faculties will give you a solid foundation upon which to build the life you desire.

Imagination and intuition work very closely together. Intuition is the faculty through which hunches and inspirations are received. Do you remember how at the beginning of this chapter I had these persistent thoughts as a little girl; I heard a faint voice telling me to pursue a certain path? I spent more time denying it than acknowledging it. And the first few times I did acknowledge it, I quit at the first sign of opposition. I am now aware that the faint voice was my intuition. According to new thought author Wallace D. Wattles, "Desire is the effort of the unexpressed possibility within you, attempting to express itself through you in physical form." I was intuitively aware of my desires from a very early age. It wasn't until I was a 36-year-old that I acted on this incessant nudge from the universe. I finally had this understanding of what I should do with my life without the need for conscious reasoning. I was finally aware of what I wanted to be when I grew up, which I had always known deep down, but I did not have the courage or the burning desire to stake my life on it before then.

My intuitive voice is much stronger today. I use my creative imagination, which is the part of our higher self where inspirations and ideas are received. Nothing inspires me more than giving birth to a new idea. I look at these ideas and inspirations as the universe paving my way to success. It was entrusted to me to breathe life into it. If the idea will move me in the direction of my dream, then I immediately take inspired action. I get emotionally involved with it and expect the image I have built with my imagination to manifest from the intellectual to the physical plane. For me, it gets easier and easier with practice — and it will for you too.

Will gives you the ability to focus on a single outcome. You must focus on the end result without worrying about how you are going to get there. Jack Canfield, co-creator of the *Chicken Soup for the Soul* series, says, "Our job is not to figure out the how. The how will show up out of a commitment and belief in the want." Having extreme focus and a solid commitment to the goal will move you in the direction of the how and ultimately to the achievement of your goal. Sarah's story is a great example of the power of imagination and will working in tandem.

Your memories form the basis of your thoughts. The problem with this is that the majority of our memories are negative. Imagination helps us to create big, beautiful images on the screen of our mind. As you visualize and focus on your goal, the end result, and become emotionally involved with your vision, you build cells of recognition in your memory bank, thus creating new memories.

Development of Imagination

There are numerous tools available to help develop and fortify your imagination. Now that you have an understanding of the faculty of imagination and your role in the creative process, the exercises outlined below will help you continue to make positive things happen in your life. There are two exercises that I like to use with my clients to help them build stronger imaginations and create big, beautiful images.

Visualization. Visualization is the process of making mental images. Genevieve Behrend said, "We all possess more power and greater possibilities than we realize, and visualizing is one of the greatest of these powers." Behrend was the only personal student of the great Judge Thomas Troward, one of the early teachers of spiritual metaphysics and the author of *Mental Science*. Thomas Troward chose Behrend as his only pupil, and she went on to teach, lecture and practice "mental science" in North America for 35 years, as well as write her own popular books, *Your Invisible Power* and *Attaining Your Heart's Desire*.

In her introduction to *Your Invisible Power*, Behrend said:

> Try to remember that the picture you think, feel and see is reflected into the Universal Mind and by the natural Law of Reciprocal Action must return to you in either spiritual or physical form. Knowledge of this Law of Reciprocal Action between the individual and the Universal Mind opens you to free access to all you may wish to possess or to be.

Your Invisible Power remains Behrend's most popular work. It teaches you how to use the power of visualization and other processes taught by Thomas Troward to transform your life. It is a powerful, yet simple and easy guide. Below is an excerpt from Chapter 1:

CHAPTER I: Order of Visualization

The exercise of the visualizing faculty keeps your mind in order, and attracts to you the things you need to make life more enjoyable in an orderly way.

If you train yourself in the practice of deliberately picturing your desire and carefully examining your picture, you will soon find that your thoughts and desires proceed in a more orderly procession than ever before.

Having reached a state of ordered mentality, you are no longer in a constant state of mental hurry. Hurry is Fear,

> and consequently destructive.
>
> In other words, when your understanding grasps the power to visualize your heart's desire and hold it with your will, it attracts to you all things requisite to the fulfillment of that picture by the harmonious vibrations of the Law of Attraction.
>
> You realize that since Order is Heaven's first law, and visualization places things in their natural order, then it must be a heavenly thing to visualize.
>
> Everyone visualizes, whether he knows it or not. Visualizing is the great secret of success.
>
> The conscious use of this great power attracts to you multiplied resources, intensifies your wisdom, and enables you to make use of advantages which you formerly failed to recognize.
>
> Genevieve Behrend

Through this process of visualization you build an image. You have to see yourself in the picture and burn it into your mind. Remember that visualization of wanting what you do not have is the backwards process. You need your thoughts to be orderly and detailed. The more detail you can bring to the image, the clearer it becomes and the more easily you can become emotionally involved with it. Focus on what it looks like, what it feels like, and what it sounds like. Once you become emotionally involved with the image, you are in a harmonious vibration with it and you will attract everything that you need for it to manifest physically in your life.

"Your vision will become clear only when you can look into your own heart... Who looks outside, dreams; who looks inside, awakes." ~ Carl Jung

Vision Boards. Vision boards are one of the most popular ways to visualize your goals and keep you focused. A vision board is more than pictures, quotes, glitter and glue. It is a tool that helps clarify your true vision of who you are, your wants and your desires. Bob Proctor says:

> The vision board holds the key to helping you create your own vision for each area of your life, enabling you to tap into the ultimate power of visualization. Using your own mental image power ... freeze-frame your vision with intention and activate it with decision.

Many people have vision boards with desired homes, cars, or holiday destinations on them. The vision board's purpose is to build cells of recognition in your brain for this new object or desire. This helps you to become emotionally involved with the idea. The more you stay focused on the vision, the clearer the picture will be created in your conscious and intellectual mind. Mixed with emotional involvement, it impresses the vision upon the subconscious and emotional mind and leads your body into action. The subconscious mind is totally deductive — it cannot tell the difference between what is real or imagined. Once it accepts the thing as real, it moves your body in the direction of your "reality" to act and move in the picture of your desire.

Evidence of this theory can be found in science. For example, take the placebo effect. Patients who take placebo pills (sugar pills) often experience the same effect as patients who take the real medications. The vision board can act much like a placebo. When you see yourself in a vision and believe in that vision, you step into the creative process. The vision process becomes the automatic mechanism to manifest the energy of your thoughts. When you grasp an intellectual understanding of this concept and use it purposefully to build your desired vision (not the vision of your fears), it becomes a process of creation and sustained purposeful thought.

Your vision board can be as simple or as elaborate as you wish. My vision board is framed and leans against the wall on my desk. It is a collage of images, pictures, power words, and quotes that appeal to me. As I look at my board each day, it burns the combination of objects and events into my subconscious mind, keeping me focused and guiding me toward making my vision real. Vision boards help to unleash your imagination — one of the most powerful forces on the planet.

Conclusion

The creative aspect of us lies in our six intellectual faculties: imagination, memory, reason, perception, intuition, and will. As you use and develop your intellectual faculties, you can tune in on a higher thought level to pull thoughts together, and plant those thoughts in your subconscious mind. By changing your paradigms (beliefs, memories, self-image) you will change your vibration, and you will start to attract to you whatever is in harmony with you. Bob Proctor said, "We have right in the center of consciousness, perfection, and our purpose in life is to work toward letting that perfection express itself." We are only scratching the surface of what we are capable of. We have more ability, integrity, power, and love inside of us than we know. Our job is to become aware of it and to express it.

I hope I have given you an in-depth look at the intellectual faculty of imagination, and how using your imagination and developing it is one of your keys to create freedom in your life. Most people react to what happens to them. You now have a tool in your hand, this book, to guide you to a place where you are no longer outer-directed with thoughts of confusion and fear. Take control of your own thoughts to control your life. Realize that limitations are self-imposed. As you apply these keys to your life, you will begin to form new paradigms that will serve you rather than stifle you; they will create ease in your life rather than "dis-ease"; they will fill you up with joy rather than weigh you down with fear and doubt. Remember what George Bernard Shaw said: "Life isn't about finding yourself, it's about creating yourself." Let's begin creating and building those big beautiful pictures, shall we? Imagine what you can do from this day on with what you now know.

> "You've imagined it. Therefore it exists... Anything that goes through your imagination has a right to live." ~ Stella Adler

Gwen Boudreau, Canada

Chapter 3

Your Memory

The key to freedom from the past.

By Nita Matthews-Morgan

> "One of the biggest lies we have come to believe about ourselves and our true nature is that we are nothing more than physical beings defined by a material reality, devoid of dimension and vital energy, and separate from God — which I trust you know by now is within us and all around us."
>
> ~ Dr. Joe Dispenza

I grew up in Argentina, in South America. Every summer, my family would spend two or three weeks in the mountains of Cordoba. We stayed in a camp with other families, and every day I would swim with the other children in a pool fed by mountain springs. This was not a typical swimming pool, with a floor of tile or concrete. Unlike built-in pools, this pool had aquatic plants growing at the bottom, and weeping willows with drooping, leafy limbs over the water. We would play chase in the water, and I would hide by swimming down to the bottom of the pool and grabbing the waving fronds to pull myself into a sitting position. I would stay at the bottom until my lungs felt like they might burst and I had to surge upward for air. Of course, then the other children would catch me. I played for hours and had to be dragged out of the water. I never wanted to leave that camp, and especially the pool. This childhood memory shaped my love of swimming and my feeling of being an accomplished swimmer. I still love to swim in deep, spring-fed pools.

Memory is your key to freedom from the past. Your memories are powerful — they form the basis of your thoughts in your present reality. Remember that you think hundreds upon thousands of thoughts every day; however, most of these thoughts are similar or the same as the ones you had yesterday. We go over past memories repeatedly, like a track on a CD, as we try to come up with solutions to our present-day problems by accessing information from the past. The problem with this technique is that our past memories are often negative, and we tend to worry about the same things we worried about in the past.

Focusing on negative memories and thoughts creates two negative effects. First, you focus most of your mental energy on repetitive, mainly negative, thoughts, which doesn't leave much time and energy for creative thought. And second, you make the neural networks stronger the more you focus on and remember something. So if you replay the memory of the time your dad yelled at you for making a mistake, you strengthen that memory. That makes the memory active once again, and you are more likely to act in a way and seek out experiences that confirm this memory. We interpret life events to match our beliefs, and this interpretive power makes thoughts become reality. By focusing on bad memories and experiences, you are more likely to create more of the same in your present reality. Of course, the same holds true for positive thoughts; they create positive results.

You may think that a chapter on the subject of memory would discuss different memory strategies. But plenty of other books will teach you memory techniques; this chapter on memory will focus on the *content* of your memory. Having a weak memory is not really as important to your happiness as the quality of the memories you hold on to. My memory for facts and figures is not very good, and I usually do not remember the names of people when I meet them, but that has not stopped me from being successful. However, negative memories about ourselves are likely to keep us stuck, because we remember and dwell on our failures instead of our successes, and these unhealthy memories can stop us dead in our tracks. Would you like to replace your negative memories with empowering, life-affirming memories that excite you and move you forward? If so, then this chapter is for you, because I am going to show you how to improve your memory so you can use it as a key to be free of faulty logic and past conditioning.

Memory is Reconstructed

Your memory is reconstructed stories. You made up your memory with your own, as well as others', perceptions and interpretations of events. You have a story about many of the things that happened to you as a child. Some of the stories you think about and retell may serve you well, and some of them you need to get rid of right now. Why would you hang onto them if they keep you stuck in your life?

I would like to invite you to be open to the possibility that some of your memories can be reworked or even replaced. Think of clearing your mind like you would your garage or attic. Then think of going shopping for new thoughts or memories that fill your mind, just as you would go to the finest furniture store to buy the best, most expensive furniture and accessories. You want the best for your home, and you want only the best for your mind.

Now, I can hear you saying, "But what happened is real. Are you telling me to make stuff up?" Let me answer that question after I've explained an important belief I have.

Memory of You as Perfect

We are spiritual beings, living in a physical body, gifted with an intellect. You were born with an image of your success, which comes from your connection to Infinite Intelligence — the creative force of the universe. As children we are more aware of this connection than we are as adults. You may not remember the magic of being a child, but you were filled with wonder and awe about yourself and the world. You were excited about learning. You thought you could do anything. You thought you were perfect just as you were.

What is it like to live knowing you were born successful and to experience a feeling of wholeness, where you feel that there is nothing to change and nothing to do to earn love? It means that at this very moment you get a sense that you are enough right now! When you realize that you are born successful, you can relax into who you are in this present moment, allow your grandest visions to surface, release the fear of dreaming big, and step into the arena where you have instant access to Infinite Intelligence. Try to experience that place here and now by remembering the *real* you, before you learned to live small. When you remember your wholeness and your natural ability to succeed, you let go of striving and you show up as your fullest self-expression. You can connect to your wholeness and to your perfection when you let go of memories that do not reflect the best of who you really are. Fill yourself with the memory that you were born to succeed and replace all the narrow, self-limiting thoughts with images of success. What do you have to lose?

Others Shape Our Memories

We have all had life experiences that have tarnished our self-confidence. You may have had experiences similar to this one regarding a two-year-old I saw in a restaurant. She was showing her wonderful twoness by standing on her chair. Her parents shouted, "Sit down and shut up." Then her mother said in an irritated voice, "Why are you so difficult?" I would have liked to walk over to that child and tell her, "Why are you so glorious and so perfectly in tune with what a young child does, so sure of your place in life?" Sometimes those who love us the most and try to protect us have lost their own connection to their image of success and act out of anger and fear.

It is not just your parents who contribute to your feelings of not being enough. School also taught you not to listen to your inner voice as you interacted with teachers, and with other children who had already lost their inner vision of success. I know you have memories of times when you felt shame and, no matter what you did, you did not feel like you were enough. We all have had those moments.

Yes, we were born perfect. Some of us spend the rest of our lives searching for things that connect us to that feeling or memory of perfection. Many of us, however, never find that magical connection again. We often die without experiencing the excitement of living free of conditioned, negative memories. We never become free to create anything we want.

You have the opportunity to tap into your unlimited potential. And when you do, you will let go of that faulty logic and past conditioning so you can experience the freedom to create whatever you want in your life. This is the easy and effortless path. This is the path of least resistance.

Some Facts About Memory

You learned in the chapter on The Mind about the conscious and subconscious mind. Memory is stored in both these parts of your mind as long- and short-term memory. You store information in your conscious mind, some of it in what experts call long-term memory, some in short-term memory. Long-term memory is the storehouse of knowledge you have collected, such as the definition of a noun or adverb, the formula for pi square, your multiplication tables, as well as the smell of your mother's perfume as you sat next to her on the church pew. Your beliefs about yourself and the world form your habitual ways of thinking, which reside in long-term memory. If you think of your mind as a computer, then your long-term memory is your software. And sometimes your beliefs contain virus codes that infect your mind, just like a virus infects a computer. You have learned these beliefs from others. I know you have heard people say these things or maybe you have said them: "I can't do what I really want to do with my life because I will never make any money," or "You can't trust anyone." Here's one I hear a lot: "You work hard and then you die."

Short-term memory is what you use when you want to order pizza; you look up the number and rehearse it until you get someone on the phone. After you order the pizza, you may promptly forget the number unless you call that pizza place several times. In other words, you repeat the information so that it moves into long-term memory. The only way to create new thoughts and memories of success is through repetition. Repeating a thought means you are strengthening already existing nerve connections and making new neural networks.

Have you ever changed a habit but then found yourself easily slipping back into your old habit under stress? According to Russ Harris, M.D., when you form new habits, either of thought or behavior, your brain lays down new neural pathways on top of the old ones, rather than replacing them. The more you use your new thoughts and memories, the more these thoughts will become habitual; yet those old patterns of thought, the old neural networks, will not disappear. It is just like when you learn to become fluent in a foreign language: you do not lose the ability to speak English or your original language. So when you are trying to deal with stress through relaxation or exercise instead of overeating, and you find yourself still wanting beer and chips at night when you are tired, remember that your old neural networks are still there waiting to be activated.

Your memory stores events that happened to you as stories. Think back to when you were learning your multiplication tables. You may remember the day you were studying the two times table, when you finally learned to count by twos. You might even remember sitting at the dining room table and working with your mother. You remember the feel of the chair under your legs and the smell of the wax from the candle she had burning to dissipate the smell of frying chicken. You store the impressions that your senses were picking up during events as well as your feelings. It is as if you have a movie projector running all the time and recording input from all your senses. Be aware, though, that your movies are unlike Hollywood feature films, where different camera angles and views are used to create a more realistic picture. Your inner movies use just one view, the lenses of your eyes and your perception.

Early Experiences Shape Your Memory

Early experiences, even your prenatal experience, shape your memory. You started constructing your memories before you were born.

As you floated in your perfect water world in your mother's womb, you began forming your view of yourself and of the world. You heard your mother's voice and the voice of your father, if you had a father present during this time. The language you heard formed the basis of your understanding of language. If you heard complex, rich language, then you were born with more ability to understand this type of language and to interpret your world more elaborately and more figuratively. You heard the tone of voice of your parent or parents and heard their music. As you tasted the food that your mom tasted through the amniotic fluid, you were starting to create your memory and story of the world.

Your birth experience was important in shaping your view of the world and therefore your memory. If your birth experience was traumatic, you stored that memory in your cells — and this memory could have shaped how you perceive events now. You do not have a conscious memory of this trauma, but it can become a powerful magnet that attracts experiences to you that confirm your view of the world.

According to Karl Pribrium, author of *Language of the Brain*, memories can be described as holograms. Remember the familiar holograms in the *Star Wars* films? We create them in our minds. When a sound, word, smell, situation, etc., triggers a memory, we project a 3-D memory in our minds as full, rich details, just like a movie. The research of the molecular biologist Candace Pert showed that the whole body is a chemical hologram. Every cell has information molecules that can trigger information in the body as memories that will determine our feelings and actions in our current life experiences. This is how your memories shape your present life and results.

The Timing of Brain Development Affects Memory

Your brain as a child was much more impressionable (neuroscientists use the term "plastic") in early life than it is now. This plasticity means you were more open to learning as a child. But it also meant you were more vulnerable to the interpretation of life given to you by the people around you. You were still developing the ability to judge or analyze thoughts because the frontal lobes of your brain were still developing. In addition, you were still learning to use language to help you process your experiences and store them as memories. You remember things better if you talk about them and sequence them in your mind.

The human brain functions at different levels of electromagnetic activity known as brain waves. These brain waves range from the lowest levels of the subconscious mind, called delta brain waves, to beta waves, which represent conscious, analytical thought. Until you were two, your brain was mainly in delta brain waves, the waves of deep sleep. You functioned mainly from your subconscious mind, and your conscious mind was functioning at a very low level. Your mind was wide open to everything you heard, so you probably accepted without question statements like, "Boys don't cry. Girls are pretty, not smart. You're not as smart as your brother."

Your brain waves began to show higher frequencies as you got older. Between ages two and five, your brain functioned mainly in theta waves, which meant you were in a trance-like state, very connected to your imagination. You still didn't think analytically and logically, and so you were unable to question the messages you received from others. Much of what you saw and heard entered and lodged in your mind.

As your conscious, analytical mind began to form between the ages of five and eight, your brain waves changed to an alpha frequency. At this age, you loved to pretend. Your inner imaginary world was as real as the "realistic" world of the adults around you. You had one foot in your conscious mind and one foot in your subconscious mind.

Your brain activity increased to the higher frequencies of beta waves between the ages of eight and twelve. During these years, you began to think analytically, as your conscious mind developed. The doorway between your subconscious, imaginary world and the rational, conscious mind was still open, and you continued to be able to go back and forth easily until you were twelve. Then, as you functioned more and more in beta waves, the door to your subconscious mind closed.

By now, you can probably see how the ideas, thoughts, images, and feelings of the people around you entered your open mind when you were a young child. Remember the important fact that your subconscious mind cannot accept or reject an idea. You may have heard your mom say, "I don't know how we are going to pay the bills this month." Your dad may have said, "Money doesn't grow on trees, you know." You may have heard, "You can't always get what you want," or "You always have to think of others first," or "Don't be selfish." All these thoughts became your memories and the basis of your habitual, default way of thinking about yourself and the world. Yes, you heard some good things, too, but as you will learn, the negative stuff sticks harder than the positive.

The interpretations of life you heard from your parents, relatives, teachers, and peers entered your mind before you had the ability to choose these thoughts. The words that you heard and the impressions that you observed and picked up with your finely tuned intuition became some of the thoughts you have right now while you read these words. Your parents may never have told you, "You have to be perfect for me to love you," but you saw them get mad at themselves when they made a mistake or absorbed their angry words when you made a mistake. Memories such as these shape how you interpret your present reality and how you see your future.

Are Your Memories Accurate?

Do you remember a day you when you might have dropped your ice cream cone onto the hot pavement on a summer day? Maybe you cried and cried and cried, according to your mom. Did it really happen this way? Did it happen to you or your brother or sister? Do you really remember this event or was this a story that was told to you by someone else, probably your parents? Think about stories like these that your family members keep telling about you. They've been retold so many times that the line between fantasy and fact may be blurred. Do you ever wonder if the story really happened the way you heard it, or if the events really even happened? The fact is that you reconstruct memories based upon your perceptions of events and the stories of other people.

If you are like most people, you would swear that everything you experienced really happened the way you remember. However, your memories are all reconstructed scenes based upon your perception and interpretation of events. You do this reconstruction to help you explain and understand your world. Your positive memories help you gain success today. Yet your memories of mistakes and failures keep you stuck. You keep recreating them as you weave them into what is happening right now and into your predictions of your future. You will read in the Perception chapter that you perceive your world through your five senses, and you rely heavily on your sense of vision. Two separate studies, one by Werblin and Rosca and another by Timothy Goldsmith, found that only four percent of vision is what you actually see, and the other 96 percent of vision is made up from your other senses, feelings and prior conditioning.

The stories you have made up to explain your experiences mean that you usually see and experience what you expect to see, rather than the reality that unfolds before you. This perception is the reason for the inaccuracy of eyewitness reports. There are experiments in which a person bursts into a room holding something in his or her hands before rushing out. The reports of the people in the room were as varied as the number of people and their backgrounds. Some people saw the person as African American, where others reported them as Caucasian. Some saw a gun in their hand, while others saw another object. The person's prior conditioning and experiences colored the perceptions of what really happened in that room. So memory is not accurate. If there are 10 people at the scene of an accident, there may be 10 different interpretations.

Memory expert Elizabeth Loftus showed that memory can also be led. Subjects were asked questions at a scene of a car accident. Asking someone a leading question such as "How fast was the car speeding?" changed the answer to reflect increased speed, while asking "How fast was the car going?" did not. Including the word *speeding* or using the verb *smashed* instead of hit even caused witnesses to remember broken glass at the scene of the accident when there was no glass on the pavement.

Now think about how others shape your memory of events. What about all those stories your mom, dad, or grandma continually tell about you? You know the ones, which are sometimes embarrassingly detailed (and now you know perhaps not so accurate). Every time a story is told, details are added from the storyteller's point of view so that the final interpretation of what really happened may not reflect the truth. Your memories are also not accurate. In truth, you forget or distort parts of the story that do not fit into your interpretation. For example, if your perception of your father was that he was a mean son of a gun, then you are going to remember the bad things he did and you may forget positive things about him.

As I explained earlier, your memory is reconstructed stories. So let's go back to the story I was telling about learning your multiplication tables at the kitchen table and recording everything as if it were a movie. To go along with this analogy of the movie, you record it, but you also edit the movie as your mind records it. You edit based upon prior stories that sometimes control your ability to even perceive what actually happened. The memory of this event can also be affected by other information picked up by your senses at a later event. In the math example, if, on a later occasion, your dad helped you with math, you may have picked up his impatience and frustration with you, and you stored learning your times tables with the feelings of impatience and frustration until, over time, you integrated both memories so that you were unable to distinguish between them, and most likely the negative memory won out over the positive.

I hope you are beginning to understand that since you always try to make sense of your experiences, you always rewrite your story. You remember the facts and events from your past that are necessary to keep the story meaningful and that fit the concept you have of yourself. You perpetually rewrite your stories — and, therefore, your memories.

In constructing your memories, you remember emotionally charged memories (both positive and negative) more easily than memories that are uneventful and ordinary, because these last memories do not stand out from all the other events that happened. That is why you might remember the day in fourth grade when a classmate pulled a chair out from under you as you were about to sit down. You remember falling on your bottom and the other kids laughing. You may also remember your anger toward your classmate. Many of the other days, with no intense events, fade into a vague memory.

Why We Remember Negative Things More Easily

Your brain is wired to remember emotionally charged events. The amygdala, an almond-shaped set of neurons, sits in the middle of the brain and acts as a sentinel or gatekeeper, calculating the emotional significance of events. When something happens with an emotional charge, it tells you, "Heads up, this is important!" and you tend to remember it more easily. It will call your attention to something emotionally significant, especially when it is negative, even when you are not paying attention.

According to James McCaugh and Larry Cahill, the stress-related hormone adrenaline helps you remember. You will remember the details of the most intense moments of your life, such as the birth of a child or a car accident, far more than you will common, everyday events.

For the sake of survival, your brain really pays attention to perceived threats, whether it is a physical or emotional/psychological threat. This is a good thing, because it forces you into action during times of danger. If you lived in prehistoric days and came across a saber-tooth tiger. you would gear up to either fight, freeze, or run away. It was good that you had these survival responses so that you reacted immediately, or else you would have been lunch. Your survival response came in handy, because you did not have to go through all of your memory files about what it meant to have such a creature chasing you before moving into action.

We react physically to stress the same way we did during the days of our ancestors, so let's put our fight, freeze, or flight response in a more modern context. Imagine that you are going to your car late at night in a parking deck that is almost empty in a rundown part of town. As you come out of the elevator and walk to your car, you notice the darkness, and since you are alone, you go on hyper-alert. All of a sudden, you hear footsteps coming toward you. You react immediately as your involuntary physical reactions kick into gear. Your heart starts pumping madly and pumps blood, cortisol, and adrenaline to your arms and legs, as you prepare to either run away or fight. The increased blood flow and nutrients driven to your arms and legs raise your temperature, so you start sweating to cool off. Your muscles tighten to prepare to either fight or run away. Your pupils dilate to let in more light so you can see better in the dark, and your peripheral vision increases so you can see danger coming. The extreme emotional reaction and the release of certain neurotransmitters brand this memory into your brain. That is one reason why you so easily remember negative things that happen to you more than positive ones.

These survival responses do not help us when they kick in on things that we don't really need to survive. Remember the story of learning your multiplication tables at the kitchen table? Even though you might have worked with your mom most of the time and your dad a few times, you are more likely to remember that learning math was hard because of his impatience and anger. You were stressed while you were learning, which increases the potency of that memory and the wiring of your survival brain. You may even have made the decision that you hate math, and your story may now be that you are not good at math. The truth of the matter is that you could have been good at math, but your stress in learning it affected your feelings and attitude about it.

According to Daniel Goleman, in his book *Emotional Intelligence*, your brain is always monitoring your old memories and looking to see if these memories match current events and circumstances, to see if you need to protect yourself by either fighting or running. Our emotional memories of past experiences affect our perceptions and how we respond to current situations. A new boss, employee, or romantic interest may do something that triggers a memory of a past relationship. Whether the old relationship was positive or negative, your amygdala will match your experience to this new one–and you may assume it will be the same. If you experienced pain or frustration in the initial relationship, you may perceive the same threat in the current one and your survival tactics kick in. You do this even when you perceive the situation incorrectly and the action of the new person has a completely different context.

You may have experienced getting mad at your boss because he or she reminded you of a parent. Biologist Carla Hannaford. in her book *Playing in the Unified Field*, shared her experience:

> I've been able to see that my difficulties with men came from emotional memories dating back to the abandonment I felt with my father. Faced with a new male relationship, my amygdala would alert me to watch for similar situations or actions. Sure enough, I would find something and could easily make these men into the image of my father through my projections.

Life is easier now, and even though we are not in danger of being stomped, gored, or eaten by large animals, things have not changed much since the days of our ancestors in the way our bodies respond. We still have to take risks if we want to grow and develop. As we step out into the unknown, we have to leave our comfort zone repeatedly, and that means our fight-or-flight response will be triggered. According to Dr. Russ Harris, this is completely natural, but we do not usually talk about it in these terms. We would never say to someone, "I am experiencing the fight-or-flight feeling." We would most likely say that we are nervous or scared.

Fear Affects Memory

Remember the feeling of humiliation and not being accepted when the chair was snatched out from under you in school? All of our past memories relating to the feeling of fear are what keeps us stuck in life. The power of humiliation and lack of acceptance is left over from our primitive survival system, where being outcast from the tribe was a sure sign of death. So it is very important for you to understand what fears you had and how they affect your present reality.

Memories based on fear and anxiety can have far-reaching effects on us. Our fear-based memories are encoded with more strength than our positive memories because of our physiological survival responses. They have such a lasting and strong effect on us that you may create whole stories, entire mythologies, around situations such as the time your brother accidently locked you up in the trunk of the car, a dog bit you, or you almost drowned in a lake.

Most of us fear failure. We are reluctant to start a new business, talk to a possible romantic interest, ask for a raise, write a book, start a family, etc., because of the fear of failure. Events in the past where you perceived that you failed can really affect your view of yourself, and therefore your results.

An event that shaped my life negatively was the memory I created when I was a junior in high school and my mother helped me write a term paper. Now, it was nothing my mother did that was wrong, only a combination of factors that resulted in my decision that I could not write. I was back in a school in the United States after five years in Argentina. I did not know how to write a term paper, and I chose a topic, mental illness, that was too broad and actually depressing. What teenager can really do that topic justice? Whew! I struggled so much that my mother got involved to help me. I don't really know how much she did, but I felt that the paper wasn't my work. So the mythology I created from that experience was, "I am not a very good writer. My mother had to help me." It took me a while to change that story. You may have experienced similar times when your interpretation of some event as a failure created a memory that really affected you.

Memories based on fear and anxiety can have lasting power in your life. The worst part of negative, fearful memories is that you can unconsciously generalize them so that you remain fearful of any future event that mirrors the past negative event. For example, if you almost drowned in a lake, you generalize that memory so that you now stay on the beach even though your kids beg you to go in the ocean with them. Maybe in high school the popular girl you asked out to the prom turned you down in a cruel way, so you now shy away from approaching someone you like. You may not start your own business because you remember your parents telling a story about a friend losing their house when their business failed. Now you will not even let yourself dream about things like the bakery or the invention you secretly want to create. So you see, you continue to rob yourself of the joy and rewards of following your heart's desire, and you may not even be aware that fear is holding you back.

Fear can have a life of its own. According to neuroscientists Schafe and LeDoux, if your fears and anxieties are not faced, they actually get bigger over time because of something called fear memory consolidation. Powerful negative memories, including feelings of failure, rejection, humiliation, and pain, get stored as mentioned previously in the amygdala region of the brain. Remember the little almond-shaped part wired to protect you that goes on hyper-alert anytime something similar to the fear is triggered?

In the past, researchers believed that when you had several memories consolidated into one big memory you would retrieve the original memory. Now, most researchers believe that you perceive, experience, store, and then retrieve the last memory formed, not your initial memory. So you continue to breathe new life into old fears, making them even bigger and bigger by adding details to them until they choke you like weeds choke the flowers in a garden. Sadly, you often do this unconsciously, so you do not even know why you are stuck in certain areas of your life.

I hope you are getting the picture that you are always creating and recreating memories, changing them to fit prior sensory information and prior conditioning. Memory is a dynamic process shaped by your prior stories, and also by future events.

Here are a few stories to help you better understand some of these concepts:

As I said before, I grew up in Argentina, where my parents had moved to be missionaries. I have some amazing memories of my childhood. I can remember skating with my sister on our patio in our backyard, stopping and eating tangerines from our tangerine tree, peeling them while skating, and then being careful to skate around the peelings and the seeds.

I remember the hot nights when my Dad rigged up an outdoor shower with a hose and cans, and we put on our swimsuits and went out as a family and took showers while the moon shone bright overhead. This experience filled me with delight and excitement. I remember the power going off and lying on the rug listening to classical music on the short-wave radio.

I remember our goat, Billy Goat, who used to eat the mulberries from the bushes in our backyard and then leave purple droppings everywhere. He used to butt my sister and me to the ground. I also remember watching movies, tying a sheet around my neck as a cloak, and running through the house acting out the part of a hero.

Now, as we already discussed, memory is reconstructive. That is, you fill in the gaps based upon your present experience and upon the stories you heard your parents tell you. So I don't know if my mother really let me drop tangerine peelings all over the patio, and I do not remember when Billy Goat knocked my sister and me to the ground. When the power went out, I am not sure if all of my family was on the rug or if it was just me. I vividly remember seeing movies, but I do not remember tying a sheet to my shoulders and jumping off furniture pretending to be a hero. My parents told me the story about Billy Goat and that he eventually became billy goat stew, but I have made that memory part of my story. My mother also told me the story about acting out the adventures I saw in movies.

As I already shared, you remember negative memories much more than positive ones since your brain is wired for survival. In addition, you remember things that have a great emotional impact on you much more than things that do not. It is possible that bad memories of your childhood can color your interpretation of your childhood, even though there may have been many good things that happened to you as well.

Your creation of new memories, and therefore your present reality, is affected by what you already have stored in your memory. If you remember bad things about your past, then you are more likely to interpret events that happen in the present moment as negative.

Freedom From Negative Memories

I want you to remember that you are perfect, whole, connected to Infinite Intelligence, and that you were born with unlimited potential. You are meant for success and for the fulfillment of your dreams. You were not created to beat yourself up with your memories or to have memories of being small and vulnerable and thus living small. Remember to connect to this vision of yourself as more than enough and capable of fulfilling your unlimited potential. This is your key to freedom.

Before you start creating new memories and beliefs, you have to get rid of habitual ways of thinking that do not serve you. You have a reticular activating system (RAS) in your brain that works like a filing system to keep the files you frequently use at the front of the cabinet in your mind. These files are full of limiting beliefs formed when you were very young and memories based upon your incorrect perceptions. Have you ever cleaned out a filing cabinet by throwing away or shredding the contents of the folders? That is exactly what I want you to do with your mind. You have to make space for new beliefs, thoughts, and memories so you can move forward and take new actions.

So what are the ways you can free yourself from negative memories to help you move ahead in life? You have already started that journey by reading this book. Realize that you have used scraps of partial memories of events and stories from others and woven them into your beliefs about yourself and the world. If you are not happy with your current results because they replay negative memories, then you can do something about them. Right now, think about something you want to create in your life. Visualize it. Are there memories that come up for you that keep you from seeing your success? Now write down the fears you may have and ask yourself: Are these fears real or imaginary? Are they based upon the stories of other people? You will probably have worries when you think about this goal, but realize that many of the things you worry about will probably never happen.

There are several processes that will help you deal with the memories that do not serve you. One process is to write down events the way you would have wanted them to happen. Writing is important in rewiring your memories to create new results. As you write, new images will come to mind and these images will bring up feelings. Feelings are part of the subconscious mind, the powerhouse of your mind. Having images of success will lead to positive, exciting feelings, which will cause you to act in a new way. These new actions will create the results that you want.

If you have painful memories, write them out from the perspective of the person you are today, which is a powerful and compassionate human being. Let the big you go into these memories and entirely change their outcome. Remember, your subconscious mind does not know when something is real or made-up, so if you consciously alter the story and go over it repeatedly, that different story will change your subconscious feelings about it. Use the fact that memory is reconstructive! Earlier in the chapter, I shared how asking an eye-witness at the scene of an accident a question just one time makes them "remember" glass on the pavement. If doing this just one time can affect a person's reality, then imagine the power you have over your subconscious mind to create new memories. Remember that your mind is like a giant board meeting, and you are the CEO. You get the final say over the minutes that will be written about your past, present, and future.

How to Create Memories

Write Out Your Images of Success. You can create future memories so that things turn out just as you want them to. Spend 15 minutes every day in the morning and night writing the vision of how you want your life to be. Write in great sensory detail, because the more detail you include, the more potent your memory will be. In your imagined reality, include smells, sounds, touch, and things you see. Be in the center of your image, rather than seeing yourself projected on a screen in your mind. In other words, be in the picture and look out of your own eyes and describe what you see, what you feel on your skin, what you smell and hear.

If, for example, you want to find a job where you are happy, write about it in the present tense, as if you are already experiencing it. Remember, your subconscious mind is just waiting for you to tell it what to believe. Your feelings are part of your subconscious mind so feel the feelings of already having achieved your goal.

Write this image often. Record it on your iPod and listen to it every day. Repetition of this image through different sensory modalities will convince your subconscious mind that it is true.

The first result that you will notice is that you feel good, and you will notice your thoughts becoming more positive. As you continue to imagine what you want in full sensory detail and feel the joy of your creations, you will start to see your vision come true as you take inspired action.

Questions versus Affirmations. I personally like writing questions instead of affirmations because questions are a way around your conscious mind directly into your subconscious mind. Remember that your subconscious mind is your powerhouse — it is where you access your feelings, and feelings drive actions. Sometimes writing affirmations sets up disbelief and resistance in your conscious mind, and therefore strengthens negative feelings and memories, whereas saying and writing questions opens a window to your belief. Besides writing out your vision, write questions such as these:

"Why is everything turning out so well for me?"

"Why have I always been so abundant?"

"Why are checks coming to my mailbox?"

"How is it that my perfect relationship is on its way?"

"How come it is so easy for me to _____?"

"Why is it that I can focus on the deeper positive truth of my ability to (make money and succeed), (find my perfect life companion), (create the business of my dreams), etc.?"

"Why is it that I have everything I need right now?"

"Why is this so easy?"

Try it and see how you like it. Repeat the questions out loud to yourself and notice how much better you feel. Make up more questions that specifically fit your situation and use them when you are feeling down and discouraged.

Questions such as these will also help to rewire your past memories. As you ask yourself questions about the present, your mind searches your memory for times when things did turn out well for you, when you experienced more abundance and happiness. This is a way of reconstructing your memory and therefore your present experience.

Gratitude. Writing daily lists of appreciation is a surefire way to start increasing your ability to recognize the endless gifts in your day. Throughout the day, take notice of 10 things that you are going to write on this list. You will soon find yourself tuning into the positive things in your day; those things that you want to store in your memory, rather than the things that are not going so well. Some of my lists include simple things like the brilliant color of a redbird that caught my eye as I was driving, the mauve raincloud with the sun behind it, or the feeling of peace I feel as I enjoy my early morning coffee on my front porch.

Developing an attitude of gratitude and writing these appreciation lists help you tune into the present moment. After all, you only have the present moment, because almost everything in the past is an illusion that you have reconstructed. So pay attention to the present moment. You will feel better as you train your memory to remember good things, life-affirming things, and memories when you felt confident and valuable.

Self-talk. The way you speak to yourself in your head affects the memories you create. You will probably speak to yourself with the same words and tone that you heard in childhood. The harsh voice in your head that criticizes and demeans you is a bully. Your tendency is to fight, freeze, or run away from bullies. Remember the stress response? None of those choices help you. The voice of your higher self, which is connected to Infinite Intelligence, may be very quiet, and you may hear it infrequently at first — but that voice is the one to listen to.

You can give names to your internal voices. Life coach Martha Beck referred to her inner voices as "Fang" and "Buddy." Fang's voice was loud and cruel and mainly focused on faults and incomplete lists of things to do. Beck described Buddy as not really having words, just feelings. Your feelings, your inner "Buddy," will lead you to what you want in your life.

One day I was sitting in my living room opposite my grown son, and I was listening to an educational CD. As I took notes, I started doodling on my paper, something I usually do during a lecture, when all of a sudden I found myself sketching my son, who was sitting on the sofa in front of me. Now I love to draw and paint, but I don't let myself do it very often because of my belief that "I have to work hard," which is something I'm still working on. My inner "Buddy" flooded me with intense pleasure as I drew him all sprawled out on the navy sofa, and I realized how I wanted to infuse more creativity into all that I do. This experience led me to create more creative, pleasurable ways of delivering information to my online clients. Just as with me, the messages from you own "Buddy" can point you in a new direction. Listen to your "Buddy." Listen to your inner voice of success.

Start paying attention to your feelings, which are your emotional guidance system. Notice whether a thought gives you a feeling of constriction and fear or a feeling of expansion and possibility. Remember the game we played as children, where someone hid something and we tried to find it while someone gave us the clue, "You're getting colder," or "You're getting warmer." Martha Beck suggested that you play that game with yourself when you have thoughts or decisions to make. As you move ahead in your life, pay attention to when you are getting warmer or colder. You do not have to know all the answers when you create something new in your life; just head in the direction of what is warmer. All you need to know is what makes you feel better and what makes you feel worse. Seek the feeling of "warmth."

Transforming your self-talk can transform your reality. Most of what you tell yourself is probably "head trash" anyway. Notice when you say things like, "I can't do _____" or "I have to _____" or "I will try to _____." You are already aware of the negative power of the first statement, yet you may not realize that the other statements also do not help you. Saying, "I choose" rather than "I have to" gives you more power. As for telling yourself "I will try," recognize that the brain hears the word "try" as negative, so it downshifts and becomes less effective. Say, "I do my best" in place of "I try hard." See which statement feels better and moves you forward into action.

It takes time and practice to become aware of your self-talk, and to determine whether it serves you or not. Sometimes you may not know what messages to listen to from your inner self. Here is the test: if your bully is speaking, you will not feel good. You will feel constricted and your breathing will get shallow. You feel better when you hear the kind, encouraging words of your higher self. It's as if you can breathe and expand into the field of possibilities. Think of talking to yourself as you would a beloved child. After all, you are a beloved child of Infinite Intelligence.

Meditation. Recognize that your conditioning forms most of the chatter and the thoughts you have during the day. Finding a way to release your mind and body from the negative drain of continual negative thoughts will help you choose how you want to feel and act. If you are always reacting to things, then removing yourself from your thoughts and clearing out your mind is a huge relief. Meditation is my favorite way to empty my mind, connect to my higher self, and remind myself of my perfection. Think of it as way to stop the chatter and feel relaxation in your mind and body. Meditation is just a process of going away from the exhausting, frenetic mind activity and stepping into silence. You can begin with 10 minutes a day, and there are no mysterious techniques to learn.

The benefits of meditation are numerous, including decreased stress, depression, and anxiety, and increased happiness and creativity. Meditation increases memory and improves focus, while also decreasing pain and blood pressure. Researchers have shown that meditation synchronizes the left and right sides of the brain, which are out of sync under stress, so that a person functions with a "whole brain."

One type of meditation is to concentrate on something like your breath, a word or mantra, or an image, like the image of a candle. The purpose is to gently bring your mind back to whatever you are focusing on so you can release the stream of continuous thoughts and judgments you always experience. *The Relaxation Response* by Dr. Herbert Benson, is a good resource for this type of meditation. *Tapping the Source,* by William Gladstone, Richard Greninger and John Selby, is another great book from which to learn focused meditation. The focus phrases suggested by the psychologist John Selby will really help you detach from your constant stream of thoughts.

Some authors teach meditation as a way to develop "moment-to-moment nonjudgmental awareness." Jon Kabat-Zinn's book, *Wherever You Go, There You Are,* teaches this type of mindfulness meditation. He teaches the art of paying attention to the present moment without judgment so that you are fully aware and able to participate in the here and now. Instead of controlling your focus, you learn to pay attention to whatever you are experiencing. *The Untethered Soul,* by Michael Singer, a radiantly beautiful book, describes how to allow yourself to drift back behind your thoughts and emotions so that you can really be free. According to Singer, you will access your hidden potential as you learn to quiet your mind and be in the present moment.

Singer says when you attain that state, everything becomes clear:

> When a person is dealing with their own fears, anxieties and desires, how much energy is left for dealing with what's actually happening? Stop and think about what you're capable of achieving. Up to now, your capacities have been constrained by constant inner struggles. Imagine what would happen if your awareness was free to focus only on the events actually taking place. You would have no noise going on inside. If you lived like this, you could do anything.

Integrated movement also helps reduces stress and opens up the mind to new thoughts and creative possibilities. According to Amir Levin, a group of researchers found that integrated movement like swimming, dancing, walking, tai chi, yoga, and aerobic activities helped make new connections between healthy neurons.

Emotional Freedom Technique (EFT). Now, what should you do if your thoughts are so negative and intrusive that you cannot meditate? Usually this means that you have a lot of negative charge around certain memories or events so that you cannot quiet your mind.

I have found great help using the Emotional Freedom Technique (EFT) to shift negative feelings around a subject. This technique consists of using your fingertips to tap on points on the hand, face and body while saying certain statements. Huge shifts can happen in a very short time with this technique. I continue to use it, sometimes on a daily basis. I have found that using the Emotional Freedom Technique can greatly reduce the time it takes to change my habits of thought. This technique also helps decrease the anxiety connected with making changes.

You can also use EFT to increase your positive feelings. I tapped for a sum of money that I wanted to create with my business and received it within a few months! Tapping cleared my resistance to abundance and opened my mind to creative possibilities. Please check out the reference section if you want to learn more about Emotional Freedom technique.

Repetition, Repetition, Repetition. I want to discuss the value of repetition. My clients ask how much repetition is needed to create positive beliefs and new memories to replace unhelpful ones. It takes a few days to create a new thought, but it takes longer to change an existing pattern of thought. New research shows that it takes an average of 66 days to change a habit. The way you think about yourself is a habit. These thoughts about yourself are just as ingrained and practiced as habits you use to get through your day, such as what you do when you get up in the morning. Habitual thoughts are neural networks in the brain. When you consider that forming a new way of thinking about yourself is forming a new brain connection that is tenuous at best, then you can understand the time and focus it takes to create habits of successful thinking. You create new neural connections when you change your habitual way of thinking about yourself.

Repetition of new thoughts and new beliefs is essential to undermine old negative beliefs. Think about it this way: You did not create the memories and beliefs about yourself overnight. It takes repetition to replace limiting beliefs with empowering ones. Charles Haanel, author of *The Master Key System*, said it best: "You cannot entertain weak, harmful, negative thoughts 10 hours a day and expect to bring about beautiful, strong and harmonious conditions by 10 minutes of strong, positive, creative thought."

The good news about memory is that you can tell a different story. Memory is something you recreate, and if you are tired of the same old story, then you can learn to tell a different story. We often let some event color our entire interpretation of our past. If this event is negative, as it is in many cases when we experience being stuck in certain areas of our life, then we do not have access to more positive memories.

Remember that you construct your memories so you can let go of the memories of the past that keep you stuck. Create new, positive memories every day. Let go of your memories of living small. Step into your memory of unlimited potential and success that you had as a child and step into freedom.

Nita Matthews-Morgan, USA

Chapter 4

Your Reason

The key to thinking for yourself.

By Alejandro Torres-Marco

"Reason: The power of comprehending, inferring, and thinking that will permit us to grow steadily."

~ Alejandro Torres-Marco

I was nineteen years old. I knew that drinking and driving was dangerous. Alcohol alters conscious awareness and the brain's ability to process thoughts and manage skills when handling an automobile. I had never driven drunk until that night. I based my "reason" for drinking and driving on having seen some of my friends drive under the influence without any car accidents.

I was speeding to make my curfew and lost control of my car when I made a left turn about two blocks away from home, and I crashed into a parked car. The insurance companies determined both cars totaled. Thanks to the airbags (a great invention of a truly "reasonable" and remarkable person) there were no physical injuries. I learned a valuable lesson that evening, which challenged my prior reasoning that one can successfully drink and drive.

Why Reason?

Knowing the reasons for doing the things you do is vitally important to your personal achievement, development, growth, and self-awareness. Just as heat is necessary to make water boil and turn it into steam, your reason for doing anything is the catalyst for taking action and doing whatever you set your mind to. When you understand and learn to use your reasoning faculty more effectively, you will get better results in every part of your life.

As far as we know, humans are the only animal species with the ability to evaluate their thinking. When we compare ourselves with our closest animal species, the chimpanzee, there is less than a 1.5 percent difference in our DNA composition. Thus, we may ask, if we are genetically so close, how can it be possible to be in such an unequal position? That small genetic difference gives us the capability to choose what we want to think about.

Here is the problem: despite our superior advantage, most people still do not know how to use their reasoning faculty to its highest potential, and the lack of understanding of their personal "why" limits their growth and their ability to achieve what they desire. Most of us do not know why we do the things we do. We just do what we do, either because everyone else is doing it or because this is the way we have always done things. If asked to change, only some would pause and ask why, and really pursue an answer. Without a clear understanding and a defined "why," there is no reason to change. Your reason for doing something is "why" you do it.

Reason versus Rationalization

Reason is one of our most important intellectual faculties, and often the most misunderstood. This is because we often misuse this mental process. Sometimes we believe that we are reasoning when, in fact, we are simply rationalizing. When we rationalize, we are justifying a certain behavior or attitude with our logical, plausible explanations, even if this behavior is not in our best interest (especially in the long run). The use of rationalization causes something to appear "reasonable" to us.

When we rationalize, we create an excuse, most of the time unconsciously, for something we want without considering the real consequences. We rationalize because we want to avoid feeling bad or guilty. We are usually not aware that we are rationalizing and believe that we are reasoning, instead. For example, there was a time when I rationalized that it was perfectly okay to habitually consume potato chips and beer, despite my desire to lose weight and become healthier. The rationalization was that beer would make me feel relaxed, which is healthy, right? Beer is made from yeast, and I had been told that yeast is good for your health. Furthermore, I was also told that drinking alcohol was good for your heart. I simply overlooked the fact that alcohol is bad for my liver and my brain cells. I also did not want to consider that chips contain grease and salt, and too much salt raises blood pressure. I rationalized that my beer and chip consumption was no big deal because I wouldn't drink that much beer (how much is too much?), or eat too many chips (but once I started, I couldn't stop after just a couple of chips). Rationalizing will always make us feel good for a while, and what's worse is that it will make us overlook the negative aspects of something. The more we rationalize, the more it stunts our personal growth and locks us in a mental prison.

Sound reasoning will free you from worry, doubt, and fear, which are emotions that lock the majority of people in a mediocre place — feeling stuck and frustrated. Reasoning is the key that will free you from personal limitations. It separates you from the thinking of the masses, rationalizing; it gives you a quick start and steady pace toward your individual growth, mastery, and achievement. It helps you discover who you really are, what you are really here for, and how to live a joyful life. You were created for a life full of abundance.

Our faculty of reasoning has evolved us from the time we lived in caves to an era where we can travel in space. Reasoning changes our reactions and limiting behaviors. It allows us to move beyond the freeze, fight, or flight reaction toward a higher understanding of self, where we choose our actions and live on purpose.

Understanding how to effectively use this faculty can improve every aspect of your life: your health, your personal relationships, your finances, your "you name it." Reason is your key to be able to effectively think for yourself.

If you ask anybody if they reason all the time, their response will often be, "Of course, we are always thinking." Yet brain activity does not always mean "thinking." Are we effectively reasoning for our personal growth and best interest? So an important part of the equation on how to effectively use your reasoning faculty is to first ask why, and the response to this question should have the personal growth component in it. My mathematical formula to simply express this would be:

Why + Growth = Reasoning

It is unfortunate that most people go through life without effectively using their intellectual faculties. We have been programmed from infancy to rely on our physical senses and outside influences to interpret the world we live in. Based on our past, we habitually think certain thoughts and act accordingly. Using this process, we produce the same results over and over again. Seeing these results, we conclude that this is all we can achieve, so we allow these results to define our lives.

Reason and Your Limiting Beliefs (Paradigms)

According to the *Merriam-Webster* dictionary, reason is "the power of comprehending, inferring or thinking. It is the proper exercise of the mind." Reason comes from the Latin word *"ratio,"* which means to believe, to think. So, would it be fair to say that our beliefs make us think and therefore reason (or rationalize) in a certain way?

Let's comprehend and reason the following: According to worldwide statistics, many people live in poor economic conditions. They have seen their parents, relatives, friends, or neighbors struggle through their lives because there was never enough money. Their conscious mind has collected this information based on what they have seen and heard, and has accepted general limiting beliefs about money. They have, therefore, reached the conclusion that money is a scarce resource.

If you are one of those people who have this mindset about the economy and money, you are not alone, and I want you to know that it is not your fault that you believe these things. Your conscious mind has gathered enough evidence from outside sources and people you trust to support this belief, and once your conscious mind has determined that money is a limited resource, you will have a scarcity belief or mindset. Then your life will, without a doubt, reflect scarcity. The subconscious mind will follow the orders given to it by the conscious mind. It will then make your body act and produce results in your life accordingly. Your subconscious mind will accept any thoughts created and accepted by your conscious mind, and the more emotion you invest in these thoughts, the more they will be fixed in your mind. This reflects the great power of the mind.

There is one very important thing to consider regarding the mind:

reasoning is achieved within your conscious mind with a tremendous influence from the subconscious mind, which is built through your past experiences. Your subconscious mind, as stated above, can only accept thoughts, conclusions, and statements; it cannot reject, analyze, or change an established belief. So if you have beliefs about scarcity, your subconscious mind cannot change this belief, and will bring it up every time the subject of money arises.

Once a general thought is set in your subconscious mind, the only way to change it is to establish a new thought to replace the old one– and this can only be done in your conscious mind through new knowledge and understanding. To do this, you must study and understand how your circumstances have created your beliefs. In doing so, you will then be able to change your thoughts and results. You need to reverse your thoughts of scarcity by questioning those beliefs. Once you understand the truth, which is that we live in an abundant world, you can imprint this new belief into your subconscious mind. Once it is imprinted in you, you will then act according to your new belief to create new conditions and circumstances, and achieve new and better results. Sound simple? It is, but don't let the simplicity fool you. While the idea is simple, It takes courage and persistence to change your thoughts.

Is it possible? Without a doubt! With courage and persistence, you can master the process and routinely apply your new beliefs. Earl Nightingale said, "Succeeding takes time, it takes dedication, 100-percent commitment, and creative thought."

Limiting beliefs are your worst enemies for growth. We all operate from our beliefs. Since your reasoning is based on your knowledge and beliefs, the results of your actions will continue to be the same until they are changed. Yes, your limiting beliefs or paradigms must be replaced for you to grow and achieve. There is no way that someone can achieve different results, acting from the same beliefs.

The best and most fulfilling way to establish new beliefs in your subconscious mind is through studying, gaining new knowledge and understanding. To create beliefs that serve you and will transition you from your present situation to a better one, you need to analyze already-established paradigms in your subconscious mind. Take one of these beliefs regarding a subject you want to improve upon and start breaking it down into smaller pieces. Carefully analyze where it has originated. What results are you achieving by using it? How is it that you obtained this belief? What is the good, or not-so-good, in it? Does this belief serve you and your highest potential? You will be surprised at how analyzing your belief on a specific subject enables you to think of ways to improve it. You will start turning bad into good, and good into better. Once you start reasoning in this fashion, you will change your existing paradigm and achieve better results.

We all understand that we must act in a certain way to avoid doing things that will result in negative consequences. Most of the time, we don't acquire new beliefs toward growth until we try new behaviors, applying trial and error for better results. For example, you might consciously know something and understand it, and yet something subconsciously has not developed enough to help you avoid unwanted results. This might not change until you learn it through your own experience.

Let's go back to my story at the beginning of the chapter. Can you see how these beliefs about drinking and driving resulted in a negative consequence? I understand you might think that I didn't use any reasoning in this case, and I have to agree with you. I rationalized instead. Let's examine why:

If acknowledging the indisputable truth that driving with a certain level of alcohol in your body is against the law, and is enough reason not to drive drunk, then the mere knowledge of the law should have stopped me. However, what we know and what we actually do can be complete opposites. I had observed that my friends had driven drunk without accidents, so I rationalized that nothing would happen to me if I drove drunk that first time. I didn't consider other factors, such as my speed and the level of alcohol in my blood. My thinking was, "It hasn't happened to my friends, so it won't happen to me. After all, I'm too smart to let something like that happen to me." All of these factors combined only increased the risk that something would go wrong.

The common belief that we learn only from our own experiences does not have to be true. There is always a better and easier way to learn and understand and, therefore, grow. As author Brandon Mull states, "Smart people learn from their mistakes, but real sharp ones learn from the mistakes of others." When our subconscious mind is trained in the most effective way for our own growth, we begin to understand and find what we need to live our life on purpose.

Stay focused on the "why" of everything you do, and by all

means, avoid rationalizing.

Reason + Attitude = Good Results

Your attitude is driven by the way you reason. Attitude is what I define to be a five-star process for achievement.

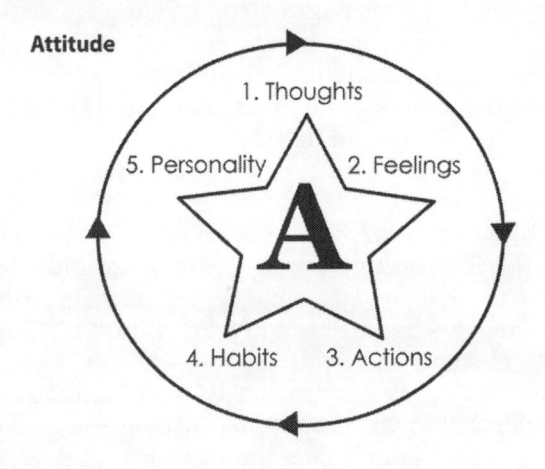

Attitude

1. Thoughts
2. Feelings
3. Actions
4. Habits
5. Personality

Every point of this star represents one component of your attitude: thoughts, feelings, actions, habits, and character. Remember the Stickperson in The Mind chapter? Your thoughts create feelings, and your feelings create actions. Your reasoning, or rationalizing, determines the way you act, and your actions always create your results. The more you repeat certain actions, the easier it is for them to become habit. Once your habits are developed, your character or personality (the combination of qualities that distinguishes you as an individual) is set. This usually happens around our mid-thirties. If you stop learning and growing then, your attitude is also set.

Results driven by rationalizing will always lead you to conformity. Rationalization is strongly determined by a lack of sound reasoning and by our sets of limiting beliefs, which have been created by our past conditions, circumstances, and environment. As we go through life, we meet and become friends with people who match our beliefs and points of view. The more we confirm these beliefs by interacting with people who act and behave the way we do, the more we get attached to them, and we finally end up stuck in a certain way of thinking and being, being less and less likely to open up to new ideas and facts, and so never achieving our desired results.

The more situations you find in life where your thinking is challenged, the more you will be able to develop your reasoning faculty and expand your mind. And when you expand your mind, there will be a shift in your attitude. The more you allow yourself to feel uncomfortable, the more you grow. The idea is to eventually find yourself being comfortable with being uncomfortable! I am talking, of course, about growing pains and discomfort while maintaining one's integrity.

More often than not, you may find yourself in an uncomfortable situation and not be aware that this is an opportunity for growth. You have probably been locked into certain situations for so long that you have begun to believe that your point of view about the situation is the universal truth. This is when we take a position and fearlessly defend it as if we were defending our own lives. This behavior is the cause of many conflicts, not only between individuals but also among groups, communities, and even countries worldwide. So whenever you find yourself thinking that you have the universal *absolute* truth based on your knowledge and experience, use your reasoning faculty, and understand that others have their own "truths" based on their own knowledge and experience. It is so important to make an effort to understand others, or at least to understand where their views and beliefs come from. Great and wise leaders are thinkers; they use this mental ability to think outside of their own experiences and become objective observers of their world.

How do we begin to shift from using our rationalization process to applying our reasoning? The answer is in our ability to be open to different perceptions and possibilities. I am convinced that exploring different possibilities will permit us to grow by our unique ability to choose. If there are no options, there will be no choice possibilities. If you are stuck in only one point of view, your choice, which is a function of your reasoning faculty, will not be an option. Remember that reason gives you the ability to think, and thinking is the first step toward growth. Our reasoning faculty, which enables us to think and thus choose, used along with all the other faculties, plays a fundamental role in our ability to change our lives.

An example regarding bad attitude was part of my past working experience; I used to think that my bosses in past jobs were in their positions by mere chance (they were "lucky"). I always said to myself that if I had only applied for that job before they did, I would be in their place, no doubt about it. That I was smarter, and I had more experience; it was just my bad luck and bad timing.

At the time, my character, created by my habitual experiences, created by my thoughts, feelings and actions in this situation, had finally created my bad attitude, which led me to think (rationalize) that it was just a matter of my bad luck and timing. My naive attitude led me to believe that they were just lucky. I later realized that no matter who my boss was — and he or she could be the smartest, most brilliant and experienced person in the world — I would find their defects or create some just so I could justify my situation while maintaining my beliefs. I would continually victimize myself as being the target of bad luck. Fortunately, through studies and working on my personal growth and development, I was finally able to understand that my reasoning was based on old thinking habits that were never questioned or challenged as I faced new possibilities for growth.

Opening our mind creatively to new possibilities will always lead to better results. Opening our mind will expose us to creativity. Are you making good use of your creativity? Are you honoring the possibility it gives you to improve your life? It is never too late to start, and remember, time passes by whether you act or not. I am convinced it is our responsibility to make the best use of our creative tools whenever possible. I call this "the creative attitude." Being exposed to different possibilities and perceptions will help us create a new reality. The creative attitude gives you the ability to transform and improve your life. When you are not creating, you are not growing; you are staying the same. When you stay the same, you remain stuck in patterns of behavior that stunt your growth. While other people are busy growing, you may be left behind.

So how exactly does your ability to create fit into your ability to grow and improve your results, and therefore your life? We should be constantly creating. We are either creating a life of abundance and joy, or a life of misery and despair. Again, your thoughts determine your results. A great number of thinkers throughout the history of humanity, from spiritual leaders to quantum physics scientists, have agreed that "you become what you think about," or "as you think, so your life becomes." They might disagree on many things, but on this premise they have historically agreed. I truly believe that people who have created anything in their lives have certainly thought about it first. As I said at the beginning of this chapter, "The starting point of everything that a person has and can create (results) is thought. Thought is a function of reason." Understanding how to think, through reason and not rationalization, will help you create the life that you want. Rationalization will give you the life you deserve; reasoning will give you the life you desire.

You Become as You Reason

You may want to look at what you have accomplished so far as a result of your thoughts. There is a proverb in the Bible that says, "As a man thinketh in his heart, so is he." In order to know and understand what you have been thinking about, you only have to look at your present results. Your results speak so loudly that your words can barely be heard.

When you do not get what you want, you may want to consider that you have based your decisions on information you have received only from your five senses. You have been living from the outside in, instead of the inside out. When you live from the outside in, you habitually do the same things again and again, creating the same results. It's a vicious cycle and works just like the autopilot on an airplane or the air conditioning in your home. Both mechanisms always work as they are programmed to do. If we want them to work differently, the program needs to be adjusted. If you want different results in your life, you must start by changing the way you think by using your mental faculties.

Living from the outside in means that you constantly decide with your reasoning faculty based on the things or circumstances that are in your present environment, things that you are currently able to see, smell, taste, touch and hear. For example, you may want to go on a luxury cruise but when you look at your bank account you don't see the money to pay for it, so you decide not to go because your account "shows" you can't. In other words, you base your decision on present results.

Your results are the evidence of past (or old) reasoning. Perhaps

In the past you have said, "I cannot go on this trip because I don't have the money." As long as you believe you don't have the money, you won't think of ways of creating more money to meet your goal. Without a change in how you reason, you will habitually do the same things over again, creating the same results. This vicious cycle will lead to your *not* getting what you really want. Perhaps now you can fully understand that all your results are a creation of your past thinking or, even worse, the creation of someone else's thinking that you adopted. Now you can understand that only new thinking creates new results, and that your new thoughts followed by your new actions will get you wherever you want to be.

Let me put this process in context with my life. I majored in biology, a subject that I really liked and enjoyed studying. When I graduated, I was not able to see how this interesting area of science could help me achieve anything I wanted in life. As a result, I needed (because of my limiting belief) to create a new reality, one that could help me achieve my current dreams. I was only sure of one thing: I did not want to be in my current situation. So I started to think about what I really wanted. This act is necessary for success: you must always think of what you *do* want and discard the thoughts of what you *do not* want. So there I was in college, holding the belief that biology didn't offer opportunities. During my college years, I also became a scuba diver and later on a scuba diving instructor, starting one of my passions in life, which is teaching. My love of scuba diving took me down a different path and away from my original education in biology. When I finished college, I traveled to the U.S. and trained in Offshore Industrial Commercial Diving, specializing in underwater inspection (non-destructive testing/underwater CCTV/photography). I started working for the offshore submarine oil industry. I wanted to earn a lot of money, and I starting to realize this dream. It was in a well-paid job, but a risky one. Remember biology? Well, it got left behind.

Right after I finished my studies in commercial diving, I worked offshore for a little over two years. During that time I met the woman who, three years later, would become my wife. This new meeting had me thinking about marriage and family — another lifelong dream. So after my offshore job, I worked inland for foreign companies that eventually enabled me to start earning more money to be able to support a family. We finally got married and started our family.

What is the takeaway from this story? Know what you want, take action, and make it happen. Once I knew what I wanted (a high-paying job doing something I loved, marriage and a family), I started to take action to make it all happen — and I got what I wanted. I admit I did struggle at times, but eventually I got what I wanted. New thinking, mixed with the appropriate feelings, followed by definite and immediate actions, will help you achieve your dreams. No doubt about it!

The power of change is exclusively yours because it is within you. It lives within you through the understanding and knowledge of what is really the truth. Start living from the inside out. Understand that the truth comes from within and has no limit, and therefore the ability to reason, along with the other intellectual faculties, can help you achieve whatever you think about and act upon. This is living from the inside out.

Remember, the power to create is your privilege.

Your Paradigms Shape Your Reason

Your paradigms (habits) will always control your logic and will guide your decisions. You reason according to your paradigms; it is, therefore, very important to become aware of your paradigms. Remember that paradigms are conditioned thoughts established in your subconscious mind and expressed thorough your behavior. Paradigms are based on learned thoughts and ideas that we have not taken the time to analyze to determine whether they are helpful or not. You just do as you do because, as many people say, "That's the way I am." I use the word paradigms to describe conditioned behaviors, and of course you want to change your negative paradigms, the behaviors that constantly limit your growth, into positive ones.

Our paradigms have a strong hold on our lives. They are deeply rooted in our subconscious, and they control every aspect of our lives, from the quality of our relationships to the amount of money in our bank accounts. If you want to change those paradigms, you will need a good reason to initiate the change. Your reason for wanting something activates emotions and hidden reservoirs of power that lay dormant within you. Your "why" is the strength that turns the key of reason. You free yourself to be, do, or have anything that you can possibly imagine.

Genetic and Environmental Conditioning

You and I, and every person living on this planet, have specific conditioned behaviors. We all have been conditioned to behave in certain ways. This conditioning is programmed by our experiences. Genetic conditioning comes from your biological parents, starting at conception. This is why we look the way we look, which is quite similar to our parents. Our genetic formation is important; however, our environments influence us the most to act the way we do.

Environmental conditioning starts in your mother's womb and continues on into life through your experiences. Most people believe that their personality is set when they become an adult and that they will remain the same until the day they die. For the majority, this may be quite true, unless they understand that conditioned behavior, paradigms, and set personality can be changed through continuous learning. We have to embrace the idea that lifelong learning transforms lives. Your conditioned behaviors that were programmed during your youth and early adult life will remain as such until you develop the awareness that you can consciously accept or reject this conditioning and start developing your own thoughts and set of beliefs. The intention of this book is to free you from your limiting thinking and behavior, and to help you develop thoughts that will serve you and help you to achieve the life you desire.

Our conditional behavior, paradigms, and set personalities can be changed through continuous learning. We have to embrace the idea that lifelong learning can transform our lives. We must reject the traditional belief that learning stops after graduation and understand that the learning process does not stop until the day we die. We must understand that the key to changing our reasoning faculty and living a better life is to change our paradigms. When we continue to learn new ideas and concepts, we open up to a multitude of opportunities for growth and fulfillment in every aspect of our life.

Remember that your paradigms, beliefs, and conditioned behavior will control your logic and guide your decisions all the time. To make better decisions, you must change your paradigms. As I said earlier, this is quite simple, but it's not easily achieved. However, it can be done, without a doubt, and our reasoning faculty establishes a definite role for this to happen. Remember the old saying, "Where there's a will, there's a way?" Well, I'll just change one word: "Where there's a reason, there's a way." Once understanding takes place, ease steps in. Here is something you will want to think about: are you willing and able to change your paradigms? This question can be answered easily but only with the response to another question: are you willing to get better results? Remember that if you are not evolving through growth, you are being left behind.

Consider another thought. Are you comfortable with the way your life is right now? You can be comfortably growing or you can be comfortably left behind. Does being in your comfort zone suit you in your pursuit of growth? Beware the comfort zone, because this is where you will stop growing. You want to be always in the position where you can change your paradigms and grow.

Steve Bow, a corporate executive, offered this quote to help with your answer:

> God's gift to you is more talent and ability
> than you will ever hope to use in your lifetime.
> Your gift to God is to develop as much talent and ability
> as you can in your lifetime.

Make a choice! Hopefully, you will make the one that serves you. You are here to challenge yourself and to steadily grow and impress the Universe with the magnificence you were provided with.

Reason, Thoughts and Understanding

> "The starting point of everything that a person has and can create is thought; thought is a function of reason."
> ~ Alejandro Torres

Most people think they are reasoning when they are thinking, but not all thinking leads to growth. We have a lot of mental activity going on in our mind, and while this activity is important, it does not equate to reasoning. After all, a lot of what we do is replay past thoughts over and over again without coming to any conclusion.

Consider this: If you are thinking thoughts and taking actions which produce contrary results to what you really want, are you truly thinking? An example of mental activity is when you sing a song that you already know. When you do that, you are engaging in mental activity by the use of your memory. You have used your reasoning faculty to learn the song, and once you learned it, you stop thinking about it. Singing this song will then become automatic; it has become a mental activity. When you are inferring, comprehending, or learning something, you are using your reasoning faculty. Reading something or understanding someone's conversation forces you to use your faculty of reasoning to make sense of it.

Productive thought must be of a higher nature, a higher and better quality than simply having mental activity. Productive thinking leads to the formation of ideas. I am not trying to lessen the importance of mental activity; mental activity is extremely important and necessary. I just want to clarify the fine line that divides our reasoning faculty from the rest of the required mental activity.

I told you what I thought about my former bosses — or about two of them, to be precise. These two "lucky" ones were there just by mere luck. I had always "thought" this way about them and acted in accordance with that thought. What ended up happening in those situations? Long story short, I lost both jobs. At the first job, I was asked to negotiate my way out, and at the second one I was simply fired. After struggling with the consequences of my attitude, several months later, I got hired for a third job. Did my thoughts change? No, and I must say, however, in this third job I initially had a boss that I did respect and I thought highly of him. Unfortunately, it was only a matter of time before I stumbled again on the same "stone," or should I say the same lesson. Because of corporate strategies, my initial boss, the one I liked, was promoted to a better position. I ended up with my third "teacher," a boss who I felt and thought had a lower level of knowledge and skills in what was required to manage me regarding the market area I was working in. I clearly remember myself saying, "Not again, please! What have I done to deserve this?" My bad luck was striking again. Well, this path had to be walked again.

At the same time this was taking place, someone invited me to a personal development training, one of those classes where you dig deep into your subconscious mind, and you start remembering things from your early years. My father worked in the movie industry as a director of photography. He had to travel often and for long periods of time, and my oldest brother took my father's role, which, as you might imagine, I hated. Well, at this training event, I discovered that my rejection of my actual and earlier bosses, the authority figures I ran into in life, dredged up feelings from my youth. I resented my brother, whom I did not respect as my father and authority figure. All my reasoning was blurred by this single experience and resulted in these rationalized thoughts, poor attitude, and ignorant, destructive relationships.

I was so blessed to find this out! I realized I had created my working environments in my mind. When I realized it was my paradigm that created my feelings, I made a huge change for the better. I finally started reasoning, instead of rationalizing. Rationalizing again in this job was going to make me fall into the same mistakes again without really understanding why. Yes, reasoning through understanding gave me the key to freedom from these repeated mistakes. I ended up having a great friendship with my third and final boss. I finally learned the lesson and moved on. Now I have a distributorship of the products from this last company I used to work for, and business is steadily growing.

The process of reasoning can take you toward better results and growth. Look at your results to determine if you are using effective reasoning. When you "think" in a certain way about a situation, which is not helping you achieve better results — are you really thinking? If you are not growing, you are only having mental activity!

Now we can define reason as "the power of comprehending, inferring, and thinking that will permit us to grow steadily."

Reason and Logic

We often think of logic as a synonym for reason; however, logic is a function of our reasoning. Furthermore, logical thinking assumes an important role in sound reasoning. I define sound reasoning as effective and efficient thinking that will help you grow. So if our paradigms affect our logic, which they do, our paradigms (specifically, negatively conditioned behavior) must be changed to develop sound reasoning. To have sound reasoning, we need to ask ourselves, does this thought help me grow?

A great example of this is, "change your actions, change your results." This complies with both rules; it is valid and one hundred percent true. This is also validated by the natural Law of Cause and Effect. Doing the same thing over and over will never change the end result. James Allen said, "Men are anxious to improve their circumstances, but are unwilling to improve themselves; they therefore remain bound."

The majority of people do the opposite: they take the same actions and expect a different result. This premise is illogical, yet many people unconsciously act in such a way. Rationalization plays a major role in this repetitive, illogical activity. We often act to maintain the status quo, achieve the same results, and then blame others when our desired results haven't been achieved. This is rationalizing as victims do, blaming others for their own mistakes. Keep in mind that victims never fulfill their potential. Being a victim defies logic and the development of being all that you can be. We are the only one responsible for our own results. By the way, Albert Einstein defined insanity as doing the same thing over and over again and expecting different results.

Reason and Decision-Making

Reasoning plays a huge role in the decision-making process. Reasoning helps you make sound, intelligent choices. Decision-making is your ability to make a choice from two or more options either encountered or generated. As simple as it might sound, decision-making is about making a choice among alternatives based upon the facts and information you have at the time. After you make your choice and act on it, you will attain a certain result. As you develop your reasoning faculty, you will make better choices and achieve your desired results.

To make effective decisions it is helpful to have your preferences and values well defined; otherwise, doubt and worry interfere in the process, and your reasoning will not be as clear and certain to make the best decision.

Growth is all about making better decisions each time. It is important to evaluate the situation and make your decision without hesitation. It is better for you to make a quick decision based on your

Your Reason

present knowledge (even if you don't like the result afterwards) than not make a decision at all. Yes, it is absolutely better for you to make a decision and fail than to never decide. Failure is an important part of the growth process. Indecision is one of the worst enemies against personal growth and development.

You may have experienced a time when you felt stuck and you didn't know what to do. Tell her, don't tell her; ask him, don't ask him. Do it now, better tomorrow; invest in it, don't invest. Make the call, don't make it; buy it, don't buy it. The list goes on. The main reason for not moving is *fear*, the fear of not getting the expected result. You may say, "What if I make a decision that is wrong?" Well, if this is the case, open a bottle of champagne and thank yourself for the decision to experience new learning. Now you will have new input for decisions you will make in the future. Otherwise you would be back at the previous point without the required learning experience. Do not deprive yourself of the excellent experience of failing by not making a decision because the results at the end of this learning experience will give you an exquisite flavor that no meal will ever do. Fear is not a choice — it is a state of mind, an emotion that paralyzes. It can be defeated every time with hope, faith and understanding.

I am not suggesting you make irrational decisions. I am saying that based on your knowledge and the situation, it is not only reasonable, but important to make mistakes to learn and grow.

Decision-making will always be easier by answering the question: "What do I really want?" The rest is finding the courage driven by your will to take action.

Reason and the Law of Cause and Effect

"Shallow men believe in luck, wise and strong men in cause and effect." ~ Ralph Waldo Emerson.

You can rationalize that events happen to you because of good or bad luck, or because you reason that you are the cause of your results. My belief is that I am responsible for my results. This belief led me to becoming the owner of an excellent business. I used to work for a fiberoptics telecommunications manufacturer — remember my third boss? Because of worldwide market circumstances and conditions, I was kindly asked to leave my international sales manager position. After being laid off, the manufacturer had offered to give me full support in becoming their distributor.

A few weeks passed, and I have to admit I struggled! Bills kept coming in as usual. Nevertheless, I had to go ahead no matter what. I decided to start a small manufacturing assembly line in my garage, putting together the fiberoptic cables to their connectors. I found out that the market was in need of quality products that preferably were locally made, customized to different types and lengths, and delivered immediately. Most established distributors carried product stock at basic standard lengths. In order to acquire different lengths, which did not match the available stock, customers had to wait at least three weeks. They also had to pay the extra fee for expedited shipping and delivery, too. I started the assembly of fiber-optic "jumpers" for the telecommunications industry locally in Mexico. I now proudly deliver to different countries on the American continent. And I must say, it was a healthy, growing business that paid for quite a few expenses.

What made my situation work? I figured out how to properly service the market's needs. Satisfied customers then asked for me to supply end-to-end solutions, and I grew my business. I reasoned that I could use the same process I used with my first line of products, and then added related fiber-optic products. My business is doing better all the time.

Some might suggest I had good luck regarding my business experience, which was *my* old paradigm and way of thinking. I know now that it was the Law of Cause and Effect in action. Luck means good or bad fortune in life caused by chance and attributed to superstition. Luck had nothing to do with it. It was a combination of my reasoning, my certainty that I could do it, and making decisions. Some decisions were wrong, yet they helped guide me in a new direction, and some decisions were right; both definitely contributed to my personal growth and success.

Some believe that luck comes when preparation meets opportunity. Is this really by chance? Voltaire defines luck as "the known effects of unknown causes." In Buddhism, the view that was taught by Gautama Buddha said, "All things which happen must have a cause, either material or spiritual, and do not occur due to luck, chance or fate." Nothing ever happens by accident or chance, everything happens for a reason, and as Wallace Wattles wrote in *The Science of Get-*

ting Rich, "...people get rich by doing things in a certain way." Forget about luck.

Reason and Neuroscience

Science analyzes, explains and determines how people use reason and their defense mechanism of rationalization to act as they do. While I won't go into much scientific information regarding why we behave as we do, I do feel it is very important to understand how these behaviors are built within you.

Neuroscience has determined that the neural pathways that you have built within your brain during your life make you reason and act as you do (conditioned behavior). You have probably heard the saying that, "neurons that fire together, wire together." Neurons are brain cells that, by electrochemical means, transmit and process all information that comes in from your five senses. The term "fire together" indicates that one neuron passes the information to another one, and this one to the next, and so on. The term "wire together" means that the neuronal information transmissions, when repeated over and over again, will start making these interconnections (synapses) stronger, and like a strong electrical wire, will rarely be broken, and hardly forgotten. Your conditioned behaviors, both uplifting and limiting, also referred to as habits, are set this way. And when emotions are involved, these interconnections get stronger, even if you are not thinking about them, making you act unconsciously and giving you the same results you have received in the past.

Understanding this process is the first step for change. Why? Because through knowledge, you will understand how to weaken these interconnections and create better ones. There are two ways to do this: first, stop thinking about them, and second, whenever the memory arises, immediately change it to its polar opposite. Simply stop the recurring limiting memory by changing it to something completely different. For example, if you are thinking about how you constantly struggle to make ends meet, then each time this thought comes up, start thinking that you are a billionaire, and get emotionally involved with the idea. Create the required scene in your mind to make this happen. The more you do this exercise, the more you will weaken the limiting thought by building a new and uplifting image. With persistence, it will soon become your new behavior and, eventually, your new reality. You could even write yourself a check for one million dollars and pull it out of your pocket, feeling joyful every time this negative thought comes into your mind.

Actions are very important in this process of change. Act completely different from the way you have acted so far. Change your attitude! Be illogical. Once you accomplish this, everything related to this specific habit or paradigm will be downhill and easy. This is why I enjoy saying, "Once understanding takes place, ease steps in." You have just read about the Law of Cause and Effect, which means that different causes will produce different effects. Attitude is the cause, and your results are the effects. If you want to succeed in life, continually seek better results by changing your attitude accordingly. Rewire paths of rationalization for appropriate reasoning. Rewire paths of addiction to worry, doubt and fear with pathways of confidence, trust, hope, faith, and courage. You will always get back what you put into life. It's like the echo in a cavern, what you shout out will always bounce back. When you perform in better ways, life gives us back greater results. Life is the mirror of our thoughts. "Environment is but our looking glass," said James Allen, when expressing the idea that "the mind is the master power that molds and makes."

You are not a prisoner of your attitude, chained to it for your whole existence. Not knowing what you now know. The very fact that you are alive and have access to the information in this very book provides enormous opportunity to change and restructure your attitude. You may have already discovered that the first thing you want to change is your attitude, your five-pointed star. First, you change the way you think, then the way you feel, then the way you act. You are creating new habits, which will eventually create the new personality and successful life you want. You can build a greater future with your new set of thoughts.

Neuroscience states that the brain is a reflection of your environment. You take in information from the environment through your physical senses, and this information becomes your thoughts. You will never be able to think beyond your environment to create what you want unless you use your mental faculties to have different thoughts.

For example, let's say you want to get rid of your few extra pounds of body fat. Every time you see yourself in a mirror and think about your extra weight, you are "firing and wiring" those neural connections of how your physical body looks. You may not be able to stop looking at yourself in a mirror, but what you can do is this:

- Immediately, and as many times as possible, *imagine* the figure you want to really have, and this will start the creation of new neurons in your brain with this image, that through the *repetition* of this *thought* will get stronger and stronger.
- Every time the thought "overweight" comes to your mind, *affirm* to yourself that you are in the process of achieving this figure, and imagine again your ideal figure. This will constantly "fire and wire" the newly created brain cells (neurons), making them stronger. Also start changing your language so that you're not talking about "losing" weight because you're programmed to find what you lose. Instead talk about "releasing" the weight.

You may be asking, Is this all I have to do? Certainly not. There are a few more steps that are necessary:

- *Act* in alignment with these new thoughts. Be congruent. How? Eat healthy food, increase your metabolism through physical activities (e.g., take the stairs not the elevator), do aerobics, start walking every day, run, do yoga, swim, or do whatever physical activity pleases you most. Move your body!
- While you are eating healthy food or doing your physical activity regularly, imagine your ideal figure.
- Make advanced decisions. If you know that eating those extra portions of bread, cake, or any other food your doctor or nutritional coach has told you not to, commit yourself in advance that eating non-healthy foods will not be in your selection of foods so the next time these foods get in your way, you have already decided that you will not eat them, period.
- Find out more through experts in the field: what are you emotionally replacing in your life with the non-healthy food you eat? If it's not a physical disorder, there could be an emotional disorder. Learning the answers will help you to understand if these extra pounds are just a bad, easy to replace habit, or

if there is something deeper going on within you. Remember, "Once understanding takes place, ease steps in."
- Spend time with people who live a healthy lifestyle, those who have healthy eating habits and include physical activity as part of their daily routine.

Please note that I am not trying to tell you that you should never eat or drink something unless your physician or nutritional coach tells you to, but when you do eat something indulgent, be conscious of your decision and use moderation. Enjoy treating yourself for staying on track with your desired goal.

Let's discuss strategies to break those negative pathways you may have with money. The steps are basically the same as above, but with some minor differences:

- Every time you see yourself in a financially stressful situation(s), imagine the financial environment that you want. Focus on getting in a better financial position. You will immediately start "firing and wiring" to create those neural connections of your new truth.
- Write in detail your new financial situation. This will reinforce the newly created neurons in your brain, which through the repetition of re-reading will get stronger and stronger. Carry a copy with you in your wallet or purse, to have on hand, to remind you of your desired financial situation.
- Every time the thought of "financial stress" comes to your mind, affirm to yourself that you are in the process of achieving this new financial status, and imagine again your ideal financial situation.
- Be alert to the signals that begin to "appear" in your life, like new people and new situations you come across. Be aware of the new opportunities that your actual job or business will present you with. These signals will give you ideas that you were not aware of before.
- Act in alignment with your present situation. You need to be physically congruent with your actual financial situation. How? Well, although you are creating new neural pathways through new thoughts, you must straighten out your finances at the same time. For example, make a plan to get yourself out

of debt as soon as possible if this is your case. This will aid your new thoughts, because you are now in the process of achieving your new financial environment. To get to the top of the ladder, you must climb the first rung, right? Do not run out to buy a new car because you have created a new image of wealth. Be reasonable; nevertheless, project what you desire on the screen of your mind as many times as possible. (It wouldn't hurt to go sit in your dream car, though, to get a feel for what your new financial future will smell and feel like.)

- Find out what your purpose in life is. Understand your natural abilities, both intellectual and physical. Strengthen them. Find out how they can give you a better financial life. More than likely, these abilities will be in harmony with what you love doing the most, your passion and purpose in life. When you act upon them, they will bring you happiness and will give you, within time, the required financial resources to live a complete and fulfilling life. If these talents do not give you the required financial resources, create other sources of income. It can certainly be done. Providing service to other people is in direct proportion to earnings: more service, more earnings.
- Study, learn, and gain knowledge continuously throughout your new life. Make learning a habit. The person who doesn't read is no better than the person who doesn't know how to read.
- Be persistent but patient. Most of us want to begin practicing and living this new mind set and get rich within a few months. As much as I would love to tell you that you can do this quickly, it will take time. However, I can assure you this: the more time you take to act on it, the longer it will take. For goodness' sake, how long have you been thinking otherwise? Patience and persistence. My uncle Fernando, my mother's brother, spent ten years steadily buying a lottery ticket, until he finally won and achieved huge financial freedom. He had a regular job during this whole time. How much time does a dream need to take form in this physical reality? Only those with persistence, belief and the readiness to receive it know the answer.
- Always do the best you can in every activity you do. Train

yourself to do your very best every time. This will build the required attitudinal habit (neuronal path) required for achievement. Your compensation is directly proportional to your ability.
- Make advanced decisions. If you know that watching TV will not help you grow, decide in advance not to waste your time in this activity, or in any other that will take you off track.
- When in business, think, feel and act harmoniously with ethics and integrity. Play by the rules and know that the boomerang will come back to you sooner or later. You will without a doubt reap what you sow.
- Find out your predominant thoughts about money. Understand how your relatives and friends think about money. Do they think that money is difficult to earn, that it is a scarce resource, or that it is reserved for the privileged? By doing this, you will easily find out how your subconscious mind is programmed. As I said before, "Once understanding takes place, ease steps in."
- Hang out with people who have abundant thoughts regarding money as part of their habitual behavior.

You can use a similar approach to eliminate any negative conditioned behavior. I can summarize it in two general steps:

1. Think constantly about the new image of what you want to transform in your life, and take disciplined and persistent action to gradually get there. You can start creating your new neural pathways today! It will always be up to you, no one else. Your rationalizing thoughts will tell you, "You can start tomorrow; today is not the day." Fortunately, you can change this rationalization impressed in the cells of your body by creating new, reasonable thoughts in your conscious mind. This will weaken the old conditioning, permitting you to grow.
2. Start immediately. Remember that the starting point of everything is thought.

Your reasoning capability is usually developed by the age of 25. During your adolescent years, you develop your reasoning ability through trial and error. By your mid-to-late 30s, you have cemented your identity, and your personality. Usually at this age, you stop learning because you have set programs. You are neurologically wired to be who you are. You have also established a comfort zone for your feelings. If something makes you feel differently you will most likely reject it, because you have your programs already set and there is little or no room for the unknown. Despite this, know that it can be changed. The brain's plasticity will permit it. You can always reshape your old limiting patterns of behavior into new thoughts and beliefs that serve you. Always!

Neuroscience has established that every time you think, you produce a chemical and this produces feelings. So however you feel, you will be thinking, and however you think, you will be feeling. This process produces more chemicals, so when you think the same as you always think, you are producing more of the same chemicals. Therefore, you feel the same as you always have. Your feelings create your attitude and ultimately your actions and results. After always having a recurring behavior, for example worrying for several years, you will condition your body and then the body conditions the mind! How? The trained or addicted cells in the body send a message to the brain through the spinal cord to think the way it has always thought in the past, which produces again the chemicals needed by the addicted cells.

Your emotional reactions release chemicals like dopamine and serotonin to name a couple. If the same emotions continually occur, they eventually become part of your personality. These chemicals are called neurotransmitters. The continued production and use of these neurochemicals guide and direct the way you think. Your perception of reality is different from that of other people because you have had unique experiences, which have produced different chemicals. Have you ever met elderly people who have nothing to worry about, but they worry anyway? They worry because they are chemically conditioned to worry; their cells hunger for the chemicals they have been fed through years and years of worrying. Chemicals that are created by the worrying are constantly being released; therefore, worry will always be present unless a major change occurs.

There are only two ways to change the strong neural pathways of thoughts and feelings that guide our lives: an event with a heavy emotional effect, such as death or divorce, or repetition of thoughts that oppose these neural pathways. One of the most important principles of learning is repetition, and this repetition must be charged with the appropriate dose of true emotions to start an effective and permanent change in behavior. Learning happens when new neural connections are made. Once you understand how to change your reasoning, your pathway will be easier and you will be free to create a better life.

Reason and Negative Thinking

Have you ever stopped to think about why television, radio, or any other form of information media relays bad news? Because it is so appealing! It is very normal for us to focus more on negative events than positive ones because we have an almond-shaped mass of neurons located in the brain called the amygdala, which processes memory and emotion. When we experience an event or situation with an emotional charge, the amygdala calculates its emotional significance and detects anything which may be threatening to us. This is a vital, and amazing, built-in defense mechanism, since it lets us know about anything that is potentially harmful to us, and we can then take the required actions to protect ourselves. The disadvantage of this instinctive fear-based reaction is that when we focus our attention on the negative, it makes us incapable of seeing the positive. So when we hear about the downturn of the economy, or the upheaval in other parts of the world, we give our attention to it and, if we are not consciously aware, this negativity from outside sources could become a major contributing factor to our daily thoughts and thinking habits.

Our experiences, both good and bad, create our memories. Every time something looks like a negative past experience, we instinctively avoid it. The amygdala processes the negatively charged situation and we take action based on fear. In worst case scenarios we freeze. While the instinct of fear is normal (and in some occasions it can even protect your life), most of the fear we experience is a misconception. It is based on our limiting paradigms. Developing your reasoning faculty will help you determine when your fear is based on a limiting belief that blocks your pathway to personal growth. As you become aware of your limiting paradigms and work through them, you will begin to respond to situations instead of reacting to them, and you will grow exponentially!

The Importance of Reason in Education

Most of us have been trained to take a certain approach to education. If you are like me, you were taught that success comes from going to college and perhaps specializing in a particular field. Your parents, caregivers, and teachers educated you the best way they knew how, based on their upbringing. Consider this: what about using your reasoning faculty and questioning the way you were raised? Was it the right way for you? Does it serve you today in helping you reach your goals and desires?

I was born and raised in a typical Catholic family in the 1960s. Being the sixth of nine children, I was raised to believe that the man should go out to work and bring home the money, while the woman stayed home taking care of the household chores and the family. Since I was a teenager, I really disliked the fact that my mother was our family's maid. At times it was clear to me that she regretted it, but that was the way she was educated and she accepted the role. Nevertheless, there was something deep within that told her it was no way to live. Subconsciously, I knew I did not to want a wife like my mother. However, as a man "educated" the way I was, I expected to be "served" as my father was.

I found the girl of my dreams. Her family was very similar to mine in terms of family roles. Her father provided financial support while her mother kept the house and took care of the family. After we got married, we both assumed traditional roles, with me as the provider and her as the keeper of the house and family. Can you see how history was repeating itself? My wife began to chafe at the restrictions imposed on her within her role as caregiver and housekeeper. On the other hand, I, as the provider and recipient of her services, was comfortable and satisfied based on my past family education. She grew and rebelled against these roles, which caused tension and problems within our marriage and family.

The battle ended when she said, and I quote, "...and because we were both educated that way it means that you do not have a mind of your own. Use it to think about how things should be and about how you really want us to grow together!" That was it. Her speech hit right where it had to. This ended the role battles. Her reasoning factor reached mine, and I must tell you, I am quite grateful my reasoning factor responded the way it did. We now enjoy our life as a couple on the same personal growth path, where we help each other to achieve our personal goals and desires.

We have all done something because someone told us to do it, or we have read something in a book, but if we don't question what we hear or read then we are not using our reasoning faculty at its highest potential. You will find it helpful to apply reason to all situations. Imagine if the reasoning faculty was taught to children in school, and reinforced at home with an open mind. It would help children learn the enormous difference between reasoning and rationalizing. It would also encourage children to question ideas that will expand their mind and help them grow into forward-thinking individuals, and tomorrow's leaders.

Reason and the Other Faculties

Our reasoning process affects our will, perception, memory, imagination, intuition, and therefore our awareness for growth. These keys, without a doubt, will set you free to create, do, and achieve anything that your mind can positively conceive. Your intellectual faculties must work together, as well as independently, to successfully achieve all that you want in life in the shortest amount of time.

Your will is the optimal engine to empower your persistence for achievement. Once you make a decision, once you have chosen to take action, your will gives you direction, and off you go!

Perception is the ability to have a point of view that leads to success. Reason will help you to understand other people's points of view. Your ability to understand other points of view will help you to think outside the box, outside of your own box, by analyzing the bigger picture of any given situation.

Being able to remember your past successes allows you to reason in a way that brings you more success. Choosing to remember your good memories will position you in the best emotional state and attitude to keep you moving forward and achieving all that you desire. This state by itself will give you the confidence and optimism for achievement and growth. Remember that choice is a function of our reasoning faculty.

Imagination is the first step of creation. Once you understand and learn to give freedom to your imagination and follow this mental process with effective reasoning, you can give form to everything you want in life. This works for everything, from health to meaningful personal relationships, from adequate money to any level of richness you want.

The voice of reason and the whisper of intuition very often cross each other. Your intuition is the guidance of your soul, and it will flow with ease once your logic, which is a function of your reasoning faculty, gives way to it.

All of these faculties must interact together, yet independently, for you to get where you want to go and achieve what you really want in life. As you develop each faculty, you will reach higher levels of awareness.

Imagine yourself always *intuitive*, with the ability to *perceive* abundance, to *reason* effectively and to direct your *will* toward your highest desired achievements, creating the best *memories* to reach enlightened awareness.

Summary

Our reasoning faculty can be developed, just as any of the other intellectual faculties. I have laid out several concepts and ideas regarding reason, so that you can understand and learn how to grow and develop this core faculty. Here is a summary of those concepts and ideas:

- Recognize rationalization. Remember, rationalization is a self-defense mechanism and will make you feel good and comfortable at the time, but it will get you nowhere fast.
- Get out of your comfort zone! Understanding others' points of view will give you a great learning experience in how to expand your reasoning ability. I am not saying that you must accept any other point of view if you don't think it's appropriate, but the basic process of understanding will expand your mind and your reasoning ability. Ask yourself the question, Where does his or her reasoning come from? Always look at

the issue from different angles.
- Be the observer as much as possible in every situation.
- Question everything. Do not take any thoughts for granted — not yours, or another's. Analyze whether the thoughts that you entertain are someone else's or truly yours, whether they are restricting you, or how they will make you grow. Practice and apply. Use trial and error. There are no mistakes, only lessons.
- Always ask yourself "why" in order to understand your reasoning.
- Be persistent. You must persist in changing your limiting, conditioned behaviors and paradigms. Paradigms mold and control your logic and, therefore, your reasoning. You want positive paradigms to control your logic to be able to reason effectively.
- Gain knowledge and understanding, and apply it. Knowledge is a great tool for developing your reason and the other intellectual faculties. You have surely heard the phrase, "The truth will set you free" — but free from what? Well, it is really from our own ignorance. To find truth you must know, and to know you must learn. Become a lifelong student.
- Take one of your limiting beliefs at a time and deeply analyze it. How is your health, your personal relationships, your finances? Analyze the how, what, where, when, and why of this belief that has been fixed in your mind. Change it through logic and action. Turn the bad into good, and the good into better.

It is possible, important, and reasonable to make our growth path easy and effortless while having fun, but beware of rationalization, because it will also make you feel good.

"The important thing is not to stop questioning. Curiosity has its own reason for existing." ~ Albert Einstein

Alejandro Torres-Marco, Mexico

Chapter 5

Your Perception

The key to freedom from circumstances, situations and events.

By Victoria Lazarova

> "Circumstance does not make the man, it reveals him to himself."
>
> ~ James Allen, As a Man Thinketh

When I was a little girl I was always amazed when I heard two adults discussing ideas, and sometimes fighting over them, trying to prove who was right. One person would see the matter from a certain point of view and the other would see it from a different viewpoint. They spent a lot of time trying to prove their point, but it was still just a matter of opinion who was correct. I wondered how it was possible to have such different points of view.

I asked my father about this when I was about ten years old. "Why do people see things differently? How can I know who is right? Where is the truth?" He answered simply, "Victoria, people see what they believe they see. If you believe that a person is decent, you will always see the good in them, and this is what you will receive from the person." I asked, "Then how will I know the truth and who I should listen to?" My father replied:

> You listen to the more knowledgeable one; you listen to the wise one; and you listen to your heart. Your heart has more wisdom than most of the opinions in the world. When you speak with your heart as your trusted friend, you find all the goodness and wisdom, and you will know the truth.

Years went by and my life was shaped by my own unique experiences. I started to form my own beliefs about life. I remained curious and continued to ask questions: "What is right?" "What is out there?" "Why do I believe what I believe to be true?" I discovered that we find our own evidence in the world to suit our beliefs — otherwise, how could we believe in our world? How could we survive in a world that we create, without evidence confirming our beliefs? We use our beliefs to feel safe and in control of our environments, and to know our place in the world.

I have always been interested in the areas of human potential and personal growth. This is why, after a successful 15-year career in the corporate world, I decided to dedicate my life to my passion, which is what I do naturally with ease and joy: helping people grow. I feel that my true purpose is to help others reveal their ideal selves. This ability has always been my natural gift. I enjoy doing it. I am grateful for being gifted with the ability to perceive others in their true essence and greatness. Today, I enjoy my life because I help others see and experience themselves as they are truly meant to be. When I see someone, I know in my heart that this person is capable of doing amazing things. Just as I know in my heart that you are capable of doing amazing things. The biggest shift that I have experienced while developing my ability to think and sharpen my perception, is that today I can find evidence for greatness, rather than finding clues for criticism. I help people focus on the good within themselves, rather than trying to change what they perceive as "wrong" with them or with others. This is true growth, and I want to share my experience with you so that you too can master your faculty of perception.

Why We Need to Study and Develop our Perception

We are conditioned to live according to our environment. The majority of us let outside circumstances affect the quality of our life and allow our perception of the world to define us. We have formed opinions, we have evidences for the accuracy of our opinions and we act according to them. Our actions reflect how we perceive ourselves and the world around us. Unfortunately, if we are not aware of that we fall into a trap. Seeing things without understanding, leads to creating more of the same of what we already have. An example of this habitual thinking is this: "I have no social life. It's hard for me to meet new people. When I find myself among other people, I do not make new connections because I don't have the social skills." This example demonstrates how our perceptions define our experiences so that our unique point of view becomes our reality.

Since we are challenging many of your disempowering beliefs and points of view about your life, I want you to consider your current perspective about the circumstances in your life that limit your growth. These limiting beliefs usually do nothing other than stop you from doing or having what you want. One of my favorite quotes is by Napoleon Hill, from his bestselling book, *Think and Grow Rich*, in which he says, "WHO said it could not be done and what great victories has he to his credit which qualify him to judge others accurately?" Then I remember what my father told me: "Victoria, people see what they believe they see." We see only what we are able to believe about our circumstances in life – and until we understand why we see in this way and explore our mind differently, we will always be bound by our circumstances and the outside world.

What is Perception?

Perception is the intellectual faculty that enables us to gather information from the outside world through our five physical senses of sight, sound, smell, taste and touch. Perception processes this information into an opinion or a point of view. Based on your perception of facts, you interact with the outside world.

Your perception forms your point of view about yourself and of the world around you. It is the key to two doors: the door to abundance and freedom, and the door to limitation and worry. As Bob Proctor said in the forward,

> We are programmed to live through our senses, through what we can see, hear, smell, taste, and touch. And we are conditioned to permit the outside world to dictate our mental state or the direction of our life. It's what we're taught from the moment we arrive on planet Earth. We have been convinced that what we can see, hear, smell, taste, and touch is all there is, even although all the great teachers of the past clearly tell us to go within, to live from the inside out." After reading and applying the suggestions in this chapter, you will be able to lock the door to the room that

contains your limitations and step into a brand new world.

Being able to see things clearly without the limitation of worry, which is almost always self-imposed, will give you genuine freedom and ultimate happiness. You will not have to worry or fret about your life's conditions any longer, because you will know how to create them. You will no longer be a victim of circumstance or a product of your environment; you will create those circumstances for yourself. George Bernard Shaw expressed this perfectly by saying, "People are always blaming their circumstances for what they are. I don't believe in circumstances. The people who get on in this world are the people who get up and look for the circumstances they want, and if they can't find them, make them."

The purpose of this chapter is to help you understand that your perception controls how you regard, understand and interpret the world around you. Your intellectual faculties are your keys to freedom and success in all areas of your life. By developing your perception, you will experience more of your present-day life and all it has to offer. You will not have to worry or wait for the future to be happy and free; instead, you will begin to feel happy and free today. How do you reshape, expand and strengthen your perception?

Individuals interested in personal growth and development through a better understanding of the power of their mind must determine whether they use their intellectual faculties in the interest of success and achievement, or as simple tools for survival. We need to move from the position of simple perception to a higher level of understanding, so that we can use the power of the mind the way it is meant to be used.

Levels of Perception

Simple Perception. What I call simple perception is driven by the instinct to survive. It is our physical experience. We have sensors that give us the ability to see, hear, taste, smell and touch. We use these sensors to react to our surroundings and to protect our bodies.

Simple perception is totally automatic and uses conditioned responses. How does this work? Both humans and animals create predefined assumptions through perception. The Russian scientist Ivan

Petrovich Pavlov, a Nobel Prize winner, made one of the greatest discoveries in physiology: He proved that animals react with similar attitudes and behaviors to situations and circumstances when repeatedly exposed to circumstances triggered by one of their sensory factors.

It was while studying the mechanisms underlying the digestive system in mammals that Pavlov noted an interesting occurrence: His canine subjects would begin to salivate whenever an assistant entered the room. In his digestion research, Pavlov and his assistants would introduce a variety of edible and non-edible items and measure the saliva production that the items produced. Salivation, he noted, is a reflexive process. It occurs automatically in response to a specific stimulus and is not under conscious control. Pavlov noted that the dogs would often begin salivating in the absence of food and smell. He quickly realized that this salivary response was due to an automatic, physiological reflex. Pavlov became famous for the term "conditioned reflexes." His research on conditioned reflexes greatly influenced not only science but also popular culture. The phrase "Pavlov's dog" is often used to describe someone who merely reacts to a situation rather than uses critical thinking.

Human Perception. Human perception is one level up from simple perception. Perception at this level uses some thinking, but without any conscious awareness of it.

Human perception comes from your previous experiences. Your experiences attach themselves to beliefs and become your point of view. It is crucial to mention here that your experiences are what you believe them to be. Your mind is supplied with millions and even billions of bits of information, and it forms images as perceptions that are stored in your memory. Your mind, through perception, triggers the need to find experiences similar to what you have inside your memory. Have you ever wondered why you surround yourself with certain people? You find them acceptable, and you do not feel the need to judge them. You simply accept them. Most of us are not aware that our conditioning affects us so much that we react just like Pavlov's dog to certain situations. Our conditioned perception is completely influenced by outside circumstances.

In order to be, do, and have more, we need to expand our awareness. We need to become consciously aware that the limiting facts and circumstances in our life are formed by our own limiting beliefs, which are expressed through our perception of the world. If we sincerely want to make changes, then we need to move to the next level of perception, where we will learn how to train our mind to create and find circumstances and events for our benefit and growth and be free from old conditioning.

Intellectual Perception. Intellectual perception is our ability to objectively find what we need by intelligent observation of the environment. The beauty is that you are able to shift your perception and purposefully use it to find what you seek. Your intellectual perception is perfect. It can always guide you to find what you are seeking as long as you know what it is that you want to find. By the time you finish this book you will come to understand that the highest use of intellectual perception is to be consciously aware that what you perceive you believe.

There is a famous story told by Earl Nightingale in his classic *Lead the Field* program called "Acres of Diamonds." The story was originally told by Russell Cornwell. It is about a man who lived in Africa. He had a farm, but he was tired from the hard work of a farmer's life. He heard that there was a great opportunity for easy living, wealth, and prosperity in the diamond business. So the man sold his farm and went to seek diamonds on the entire African continent for the rest of his life. One day, the new owner of the farm found a beautiful shining stone, picked it up, and placed it on the shelf above the fireplace. After a few months, a visitor came to the house. He wandered around the living room and suddenly grasped the stone on the shelf. He asked the owner of the farm if he knew what he had. "Yes," said the farmer, "a beautiful stone, and I have plenty of them on the farm." "Do you know that this is one of the largest diamonds ever found on earth?" asked the visitor. It appeared that the farm was full of diamonds, acres of them. It became one of the largest diamond mines in the world.

> "Each of us is, at this minute, standing in his own acres of diamonds. Somewhere in what you are doing, there lurks an opportunity which could bring you everything you could possibly want..." ~Earl Nightingale

Why do most of us believe that the opportunity we are forever seeking is somewhere else, somewhere outside of ourselves? Your mind is your richest resource. Use your perception to intelligently observe your circumstances. Find the diamonds in your own possession. Start looking intelligently at your own field to see if you have explored all the possibilities that you currently have. Stop looking at what other people have and focus on you.

We can get to the point of realizing that nothing is good or bad; it just is. Any fact is a simple fact until we charge it with a positive or negative emotion. Once we start thinking and consciously observing our circumstances, we stop being a victim of our environment and become an intelligent observer, building productive opinions based on credible facts. The people who are able to do this are the ones who make progress in the world. They are not afraid to take the next step because they understand a basic truth: everything just is. They are aware that there is always more to be seen than the limited vision of conditioned reactions and opinions based on false premises.

Those who have trained themselves to look for opportunities will automatically find them, because this is how their mind operates. When you stay focused on a desired outcome, your mind will be trained to find it automatically.

I conducted an experiment on myself two years ago to further train my perception faculty. I decided to mentally pay myself $10 for every positive and encouraging thing that I noticed during my day. I would count my "money" in the evening, thinking I would be rich. To be honest, though, in the beginning, I would not have made a living if I had to live off of that money. But this did not stop me. I started to pay myself $20 for every positive thing I saw in someone else. The more I played the game, the better I got at it. My thoughts shifted from being critical and judgmental of others, to easily finding positive things about them.

Before I understood how to use my perception, I would see the greatness in my clients, but I would also focus on the weaknesses they had to improve upon. Today I see only their greatness, and we focus on their strengths to help them reveal their ideal self. This works better, because you cannot motivate others if you do not value and appreciate them. Today, I have the most amazing people around me because I choose to focus on and perceive other people's greatness and beauty instead of their weaknesses. You always have the choice to focus your attention on what you want to find, and your faculty of perception will develop this skill and lead you to exactly what you are looking for. It is perfect.

We have to guide our perception, direct it, and tell it what we want to see. If we do not guide our perception, our environment will do it for us. We will continue to live from the outside in, feeling like a victim of circumstance. We live in a world where the majority of information comes from negativity, not only from the media but from the people around us, as well. We are exposed to a lot of negativity, which builds recognition and breeds familiarity. The mind becomes interested in and attracted to hearing bad news through this constant conditioning and training from negative sources. The good news is that not all people buy into this negativity. Even in difficult times, people continue to make money and live happy lives in spite of the circumstances. They have learned to project positive instead of negative expectation upon their environment.

Perception and Paradigms

Without our perception, we cannot survive. However, if we use our perception without understanding, we become victims of our habitual survival paradigms.

By now you understand that your life is merely a projection of your perception. You can use your perception faculty to remove the limitations you have accepted in your life; however, before you can remove them, you must first recognize them. Albert Einstein said, "Once we accept our limits, we go beyond them."

Our culture and belief systems are founded on habits, attitudes, beliefs and expectations. A paradigm is a model or pattern composed of a multitude of habits. Habits are ideas fixed in our subconscious mind. We recognize them as *physical* habits, the way we automatically do things without any conscious awareness, such as brushing our teeth, or driving. We also have *mental* habits, for example, when we think of the worst-case scenario the moment something goes wrong.

What you constantly think determines your perception and your points of view. Remember the stickperson and the relationship of the mind to the body? Your conscious mind is your thinking mind, and your subconscious mind is your feeling mind. The subconscious mind is also a big storehouse where we hold our self-image and our paradigms. Our firm belief in something represents a paradigm. The bigger (meaning more evidence and memories to prove your point of view) and older the story of the paradigm, the stronger the impact it has on your results. Your paradigms are the tools you use to approach and react to the world. A paradigm shift is a change in approach or a new set of rules or habits. If you change a habit or a belief about something, it will affect many aspects of your life. Let's take a martial arts student breaking a board, for example. She trains for years and conditions both her body and her mind for the task. When she finally breaks it, her belief about what she is capable of accomplishing can change in that moment and affect her entire life.

When you attempt to change a paradigm, you take a giant step toward personal growth. How do you know if you have disconnected from your old model of thinking? When your results are different! You may feel uncomfortable in the beginning because your new belief or habit is not in harmony with your old paradigm, yet when you notice a shift in your thinking, you start changing your mental habits.

The problem is that most people attempt to change their physical habits, yet they do not take care of their mental habits or programming; they therefore experience failure or resistance originated by the paradigms in their mind. When you attempt to change any mental pattern, be willing to feel uncomfortable. Successful people are willing to be uncomfortable in the interest of their growth.

In *As A Man Thinketh*, James Allen says, "Men are anxious to improve their circumstances, but are unwilling to improve themselves and therefore remain bound." Many people are not willing to change before their environment changes; they are not ready to improve unless their circumstances improve, and therefore they remain limited in their beliefs. People are skeptical about trying new things because they do not understand them. They are not willing to learn more, or do something different — something outside the box.

Your Perception is Your Projection

Your perception of people, facts, and circumstances is what you end up projecting onto the world. You must not let limiting paradigms from your environment and other people (the outer world) influence or alter your beliefs about yourself (the inner world). Start asking yourself these key questions: Who am I? How are my limiting beliefs affecting me? What am I reading? What am I saying? Where am I going? What am I thinking? What am I becoming? Then ask yourself this question: Is this what I want for myself?

Make a list of your beliefs and say, "I believe that. ..." Then ask yourself: Does this belief serve me? Does it uplift me? Does it make me want to act and do the things that I want to do? Am I willing to do what I want to do? When you impress upon your mind new paradigms and beliefs, you will get new results.

Your life does not get better by chance; it gets better by change and by the higher awareness of your personality.

What Do You See?

What you perceive will always reflect and resonate with your beliefs. Your life circumstances match your perceptions, which result in your point of view. Your mind gathers information, processes it through a set belief system, and produces your view of the world. In contrast with the other intellectual faculties, perception is always enabled because it helps us to survive.

Imagine standing in front of a beautiful white chair. You like it a lot, so you tell your friend, "You know, I was at the Smiths' house yesterday, and they have a beautiful white chair — it's a piece of art." And your friend is amazed, because he was at the Smiths' house two days ago, and he did not see a white chair. After a lively discussion about the chair, you soon realize that you were standing near the window looking at the front of the chair and he was standing near the door looking at the back of the chair. The chair was half white and half black, but you would have bet that the chair was white based solely on the angle you saw it from.

We believe what we see with our eyes, but sometimes we do not question the accuracy of what we see. Be sure to question what you see. Your perception is a servant to you and what you assume to be true is determined only by the level of awareness you have developed. Constantly look for the good in people and situations. What do you see?

Your Perception of the World is an Illusion

Have you ever considered somebody to be unrealistic? Reality is a matter of interpretation. At times, we may believe that people have an interpretation that is unrealistic or even delusional. But the truth is that we all create illusions and make assumptions to interpret the world around us. For example, one person you know may have the attitude that he or she can obtain anything they want in life, while another person you know has the complete opposite view about life and insists that life is a constant struggle. Both of these people have made assumptions.

An assumption is an interpretation of information we have perceived from the environment, and the meaning we give to it through our points of view, relying on our beliefs and our previous conditioning. In other words, what we see is based upon what we already know, so we look for what is familiar, then interpret the facts and make assumptions. The facts we believe to be true, however, may be an illusion. We have opinions and ways of thinking that we live up to and even fight for — but most of these are nothing but our own illusions. The perception that we hold is true to us, but that does not necessarily mean it is the truth. We construct our own reality.

Your perception is constantly working. When compared to any other faculty of the mind, you would be astonished at the disproportionate amount of time you spend using your perception. Perception is always on; it forms the basis of how you interact with the world around you. Your perception can find facts to prove the truth about your life being very difficult; however, that same faculty of perception, with the proper guidance and development, can easily find evidence that you can prosper and progress in your life from exactly where you are today!

Just remember a time in your life where you were so convinced in the truth of something and when you found out more about it, you realized that you were totally wrong.

Don't assume that what you see is the only truth. For most people, only four percent of vision is what you actually see and the other ninety-six percent of vision is reconstructed from memories, feelings, and prior conditioning. You create your model of the world. It is your reconstructed reality. Knowing that will help you to question what you see because sometimes we cannot see the complete picture.

How We Process Information

According to the founders of Neuro-Linguistic Programming, Richard Bandler and Roger Grinder (whose main studies cover the science of communication and perception of information coming into the conscious and unconscious mind from the outside world), we all process information coming in through the senses inaccurately in three ways: we generalize, we delete, and we distort this information based upon our prior beliefs. I want to briefly explain each of these to help you become aware that what you perceive and believe is only a small portion of what's actually going on. Becoming aware that there is always more than one possible point of view opens you to new possibilities that perhaps previously you could not perceive.

Generalization is the process by which we draw global conclusions based upon one or two experiences. Learning to categorize the world in terms of how things are the same or different helps us operate more efficiently. Do you remember the first time you burned yourself on a hot stove? From that experience, you learned that hot stoves are dangerous to touch. Yet just because a hot stove can burn you and can be dangerous, it does not mean that a room with a stove is dangerous. Our ability to generalize is essential to coping with the world. This is one of the ways that we learn, by taking the information we have and drawing broad conclusions. Sometimes, however, we make generalizations that do not help us. If, after being burned, I decided to stay away from rooms with hot stoves because they are dangerous, I have now made a sweeping assumption that limits my choices.

Deletion occurs when you unconsciously pay attention to certain parts of experiences and exclude others. For example, if you are convinced that your mother is always critical of you, you will not hear when she encourages you. Everything you believe is limited by your interpretation of it. Look at each situation from different angles. This will allow you to be objective so you can create more options and avoid the trap of the negative side of deletion.

The other function of deletion when processing information in our mind is to reduce the information about the world to proportions that we feel capable of handling and understanding. It is useful in one way, but may be harmful in another. Without deletion, we would be faced with too much information to handle with our conscious mind.

Distortion is the process of interpreting or misinterpreting information to suit our beliefs. We take certain facts from situations or circumstances, we form a point of view, and we create our reality according to our beliefs. Remember the story in "The Mind" chapter about the "babies" in the back seat of the car? The woman's misinterpretation of the situation caused havoc for everyone involved, until someone saw that the "babies" were actually dolls. "Your Memory" chapter discussed how eyewitness reports could not be trusted because people interpreted and distorted the same stimuli differently based upon what was already in their mind. Eyewitness reports are examples of the negative effects of distortion.

Since we all live in our own illusions of perceived reality, let's make sure that the illusions we live in are compelling and empowering. The illusion of fear and negativity exists as a reality, but so do the illusions of hope, faith, and creation. It is our own responsibility as thinking people to choose what to think and how to live.

Self-Perception

"Before you do something, you have to be something."
~ Goethe

Since your reality is what you make of it, you can change it by learning to look at it differently. Who is going to help you do and have the things you want most? The answer is, *you*! When you see the world as a place of beauty and abundance, and you see yourself as a person who can achieve things and feel worthy of them, life will mold to support you. As you create your new self-perception, it will allow you to have confidence to achieve your desires and to experience the life you were born to live.

What do you see when you look in the mirror each morning? Do you have a healthy and confident perception of yourself? True success is being able to perceive yourself as successful at any point on your journey.

The way you see yourself today is not how you were when you were born. You were born with a perfect self-image, and you felt so happy with who you were. You felt that everyone loved you; you felt no judgment, only love. Your self-perception had nothing to do with how other people viewed or felt about you.

As time passes, we form a new self-perception through our education and experience based on other people's point of view of who we should be. We learn how others perceive the world and their perception of reality becomes our point of view. Then your life molds to support a point of view that was based on someone else's perception of who you should be and not who you truly are.

Your self-perception is probably one of the most important ideas you should focus your attention on. You are more capable than you realize. We live simultaneously on three planes: body, mind and spirit. None of these is better than the other, but we cannot live a full, authentic life if we deprive any of these planes of their full expression.

Three Planes of Existence

Body. You have the physical side of you — your body. You gather information about your environment through your five senses, and your brain interacts with this information, processes it, and then forms your point of view about the data you have received.

Mind. You also have an intellect — the ability to think. You have a mind equipped with six intellectual faculties: imagination, memory, reason, perception, intuition, and will. Upon finishing this book, you will know more about these faculties, how to develop them, and how to use them effectively. Your new level of awareness will help you to see the power that you already have in your mind. Do you use your ability to think? Do you use it when you interact with the outside world to form an opinion?

Spirit. Most of us believe we are what we see in the mirror, and forget how happy we are when we connect with our spirit. Our spirit (some call it a "higher self") offers us inspiration and a place where we can experience faith and freedom. Sometimes we connect best with our spirit during intimate moments of serenity or peacefulness. During these moments, we can experience the greatness of our spirit — and it can move our emotions. Try to think of a negatively charged word when you say the word, "spirit." I cannot. I started to type the words that came to my mind when I thought about Spirit, and these words came to me: life, breath, light, love, happiness, joy, wisdom, serenity ... God.

I love words. The best teaching about words that inspired me to many "aha" moments is when I read Kevin Hall's book, *Aspire*. He explains that, "The word 'inspire' comes from the Latin *'inspirare.'* *'Spirare'* means to breathe. To inspire means to breathe into… when we breathe life into another, we inspire their hopes, goals, and dreams. We breathe life into them, just as our 'Creator' first breathed life into our spirit." This passage helped me understand inspiration, and that the inspiration I have is a gift, and it is my spirit. When I deeply breathe life into a new idea, an idea that helps me experience joy, I have received an "in-spiration" and I let go of old perceptions.

Our spirit is our gift from God (Nature, Higher Power, Source, or whatever you prefer to call it). Our spirit is our connection to Infinite Intelligence. The expression of the spirit and the eagerness of the spirit to live in your intellectual and physical world is God's desire to help you to be as creative as the Creator. The Creator has given us our spirit by breathing life into us as pure, clean, light and positive energy. The need for expression of spirit is always positive and life-giving.

I would like to invite you to perceive yourself differently, because you are so much more that you think. You are bigger and more powerful. See yourself as more than the image in the mirror. We can never be limited by circumstances when we allow ourselves to perceive more than what we see with our physical senses and are open to the truth that we are spiritual beings, having an intellectual experience living in physical bodies.

Reconstructing Your Self Perception

How do you start to reconstruct your false perceptions and build a powerful perception so you can easily project what you want to receive from your life?

All your actions, feelings, behaviors, and abilities are always consistent with your self-image. When we look at self-image through the lens of our perception, it leads to our beliefs about ourselves. How do you perceive yourself? Do you see yourself as a successful person,

Your Perception

or not? Do you perceive yourself to be free to do whatever you want, or not? I'd like to offer a couple of suggestions for helping you to become aware of what you believe and perceive so you can build your new, successful self-image.

Step one requires you to review what you perceive yourself to be. Sit with an open mind and total acceptance, and ask yourself some questions. These questions will give you a direct reflection of your paradigms and your beliefs about yourself.

Ask yourself:

1. What do I believe about my environment? Do I work and live in a calm, abundant, and prosperous environment?

2. How do I interact with my environment? Do I feel comfortable and at ease, or am I constantly frustrated and struggling?

3. Is there someone stopping me from doing what I want to do?

4. Am I surrounded with people who support and love me?

5. What do I believe about my ability to make money?

6. Do I have an abundance or poverty mindset?

7. What is my financial situation?

8. What do I believe about my personal potential?

9. Am I a great leader, parent, partner and person?

10. Do people like me?

11. Do I trust and believe in people?

12. Do I believe that my life can be easy or do I believe that it has to be hard and a struggle?

These questions will help you find out where you are and what you believe to be true about yourself. When you take stock of your life, you will find out that these beliefs are reflected in your results one hundred percent. The belief system is a reflection of your attitude, your thoughts, feelings, and actions. If you recall the image of the Stickperson and the way in which an idea becomes a reality in your life, you will find out that your results are based on your feelings, paradigms, and self-image. What you believe and how you feel and react to your environment powerfully shape your results. Which is prevalent in your mind: the fear of poverty, or the joy of abundance? Are you more afraid to lose what you already have, or are you inspired to lead the life that you desire?

Courageously answer the questions on the previous page. Be truthful to yourself. Most people will not honestly answer those questions. Sometimes we would rather give the responsibility of our lives to other people or circumstances. If you are still reading this, you are someone who believes you are the prime cause of your results and that you can create the life you want. Allow yourself to be aware of your dominant thoughts and feelings then analyze and decide which ones will separate you from the masses and put you on the right path to success — *your* success.

Your next step is an ongoing action to help form your new perception of yourself. The rewards you will receive from forming new beliefs will far surpass the effort it takes to change the old ones.

You already know what you want. Now, take a look around and find people who have achieved similar outcomes. Find out what they believe about themselves and about the world. If you cannot find them today, do not worry. Guide your perception and eventually you will find them. Start building your new belief system and say, "I believe that _____. My job is _____. I have the ability to _____."

As you build your new self-image, use your imagination to build the picture of yourself, your reasoning to decide whether it is good for you, your will to help you stay focused, and use your memory to imprint it in your mind. Your intuition will guide you in this as you build your self-image — let your heart's desire be expressed. It is about you and your willingness to allow yourself to be the person you have always wanted to be.

To see other people, you have to be able to see yourself. To feel worthy of the things that you desire most, you need to know and value the things that you give to the world: your service, your time, your gifts, and your talents. Focus your perception to find the right places where you can contribute your greatest talents and abilities. Then you will naturally and easily feel worthy of receiving and of being your authentic self.

The perfect self-image is when you connect with your spiritual values that uplift and radiate fulfillment and happiness in life. Relax and see yourself as someone capable of doing anything and being anything that you sincerely want to be. When you come to a point of deeply believing in yourself, then your perception will lead you to the environment that matches who you believe yourself to be. Your beautiful perception will find the right circumstance to support your new self-image.

It may appear simple, even foolish or too good to be true, but sometimes you just have to believe.

In writing this, I wanted to help you truly experience your greatness and perceive yourself as someone good enough and strong enough to be free. The subject of self-image is thoroughly covered by modern literature. If you want to learn more about your built-in success mechanism, I highly recommend the bestselling book, *Psycho-Cybernetics*, by Dr. Maxwell Maltz. He says,

> You are somebody not because you've made a million dollars, or you own the biggest house and drive the biggest car on your block but because God created you in his own Image. Most of us are better, stronger, and more competent now, than we realize. Creating a better self-image does not create new abilities, talents, powers — it releases and utilizes them.

Can I Really Change My Life by Changing My Perception?

> "The most important decision you'll ever make is whether you live in a friendly universe or a hostile universe"
> ~ Albert Einstein

Your life is what you perceive it to be. Your life is not given to you to live with burdens, drama, and limitations. You are given life as a time to grow, to experience love, abundance, and passion, and to create your vision and your contribution to the world.

Build a relationship with life and perceive it as your most desired partner. Be in love with life. Use your intellectual mind to gain an understanding of your thoughts. Direct your expectations and attention to creating the life you want to live. When you set your expectations, "Do not expect troubles as they have a tendency not to disappoint," as Napoleon Hill has said in *Think and Grow Rich*. Have faith in life and in you. Bury doubt. Expect only goodness and be grateful for everything. For those who have faith, any circumstance is just a circumstance. It is neither good nor bad, only another step forward. If you experience failure, know that failure is a manmade circumstance. It is given to you to learn and grow. Have faith in yourself and faith in Infinite Intelligence. Faith is the necessary ingredient for all achievement. Keep your eyes on what you want, keep your mind on thoughts of creation and growth, and life will give you exactly what you are ready to receive. Life is good to those who know what they want and show up every day with readiness of mind, faith, and expectancy to receive it.

The Law of Attraction

The Law of Attraction says like attracts like. This law is expressed through our vibrations, which are the thoughts and feelings we experience, and is manifested as actions and results (refer to the Stickperson diagram). Raymond Holliwell, a great philosopher and author of *Working With The Law*, gave one of the best explanations for The Law of Attraction, saying:

> The Law of Attraction is a secondary law of the Law of Vibration (cause and effect) and works perfectly for our desires. Our desires and state of mind also have to be set in the right sequence and process on a conscious and subconscious level to use the law to our benefit.

Our true desires are what we expect out of life. And what we expect in life is what we achieve. There is a difference between expectations and wants. Desire without expectation is idle wishing or dreaming. We often desire something but expect another thing. We have a big desire to be happy, healthy and wealthy individuals, yet we have fear and doubt within us and because like attracts like, we receive more fear and doubt.

Most often our perception is so strongly focused on what we already have and what our paradigms dictate that we do not allow ourselves to see and grasp the possibilities for a better and easier life. Do not be like most people who believe only what they can see. Use your perception to see more!

Expectation is an enormous drawing force in the mind. How do you develop your expectation? First, focus on your interest. If a new house interests you, stop looking at your old house. Go look at new houses. Second, keep your attention focused on your desire and do not allow anything or anyone to take your focus away from it. Third, and most importantly, expect it and focus on it with intensity. Integrate it as part of your perception.

The *you* that you are seeking, and the possibilities you want, already exist. Both will be revealed as you raise your level of understanding of your intellectual faculties. Do not fall into the trap of entertaining these ideas on an intellectual level only. Your true learning and achievement of freedom comes only when you start applying these ideas in your daily life. Albert Einstein said, "The only source of knowledge is experience." Knowing is not enough to get the results you want. Results only come by doing.

When we grow it creates more in our life and we move to a higher level of perception. Computer games work this way. Players move on to the next level when they complete all the challenges of their current level. Oftentimes, you may not see how to move yourself to the next level. You do not need to know how. By taking action and moving forward, you will see farther. Each obstacle is a mere detour on your journey to reach your desired outcome. Each attempt will move you closer and closer to what you want most.

How To Stay In Charge No Matter The Circumstances

Developing and changing your perception of yourself, others and the world is the most effective use of your faculty of perception. By focusing your perception to a higher level, you gain freedom from circumstances and events.

The intellectual use of your perception will help you reach higher levels of awareness. There are a few techniques you may want to use to develop your intelligent objectivity and experience the beauty and freedom of your life.

Shifting Your Perception. Shift your perception when and where you need it. It will draw you out of life's difficulties. You will release guilt, resentment, and resistance. Shifting your perception is a simple process of looking at the problem and saying to yourself, "What if _____?" Make the situation look promising and good, or at least better. Start creating a picture of the situation that works for you. Allow yourself to practice this repeatedly until you have gained the skill to do it when you need it. Shift your perception right now and see the good. If good is at one corner of the room, then bad is the other corner. Remember, shifting your perception moves from conditioned thinking to creative thinking.

Release Judgment. Everyone is conditioned to make judgments. In our mind, we want to have control over situations, people, and circumstances and expect them to conform to our point of view. And needing the world to change in order for us to be happy is probably the greatest mistake we make. Nothing is good or bad; it just is. Allowing yourself to accept everything in your life as it is will help you face any situation or circumstance without stress or fear. Release all your judgments about people, facts, and circumstances, and accept them as they are. You will move from resisting circumstances to responding and creating new ones. I always say to myself, "People, facts, and circumstances are always in my favor." And it works.

Think Big. We always think we have the biggest problems. Worse, we tend to make problems bigger than they really are. We do that not only for problems, but also for our goals. Move from this way of thinking toward thinking of something bigger. If your goal is to earn a certain amount of money and you see this amount as big and unachievable, make it bigger. Make it two, three, or even 100 times bigger. Start exploring your mind's ability to think in new dimensions. Entertain the new, big idea then go back to the originally set goal. Oddly enough, you will find that your first amount does not look so big anymore. This works also for problems. Make your problem big, then bigger, then bigger. Have fun with it. Go back and you will see that your real problem is not that big.

Focus and Guide Your Perception. In the chapter on the will you will learn how to easily hold the picture of your desire on the screen of your mind and manifest what is in your imagination into you physical reality. Your perception plays an important role. When you focus your perception to find the right facts and circumstances in your present reality, and use intelligent objectivity to discover how you can do whatever you want to do, you move from surviving to thriving. Focus and guide your perception to find the good in others, the possibilities in life, the joy in living, and the greatness in yourself. Practice this exercise no matter what happens around you. Stay there long enough and your new perception about life will guide you to find what you seek.

Be Grateful. To be happy is to live with a smile on your face that nobody can take away. When you are grateful for everything, you perceive the world with understanding, calmness and confidence.

The one thing that can always draw you out of any situation or difficulty is your ability to perceive the world and yourself with a feeling of gratitude. The attitude of gratitude will help you courageously face any circumstance and receive an increase from what you already have.

The law of praise is the law of increase and it says you receive more of what you are grateful for. It is a natural thing to want more and to look for more in your life. Do this by praising the things you already have. As a result, you increase in your mind the value of the things that are already present in your life. How do you praise? Be grateful! Genuinely and sincerely praise your life. In his classic Working with the Law, Raymond Holliwell says, "Praise with the heart is far more vital, life-giving and effectual than praise with the head or from the lips." When you can really experience feelings of gratitude, even in the face of adversity, the adversity itself will often disappear.

Learn to practice praise. Be thankful for both good and bad. Your perception and point of view, when shifted toward gratitude, opens up to possibilities and allows you to be calm, confident, and courageous. This attitude of the mind not only brings forth our desires, but it also generates confidence, strengthens faith, and builds up an assurance of the things that are not only here but those that are yet to come.

Use Perception as Your Projection. I sincerely hope this chapter has helped you to understand, and accept, the idea that your perception is much more than receiving information from your environment. What I sincerely wanted to convey to you is that you have the power to create your own reality by simply changing the way you perceive your life, other people and yourself.

People tend to see their perception as an ability to receive from the environment, which makes them dependent on other people and circumstances. Your perception is not only your unique internal representation of the world but also a projection of your life. You find evidence for your perceptions and beliefs about your life's conditions and you project them as reality. Use your mind actively and intelligently and start seeing your perception as your ability to choose what you experience in life.

Focus your attention on the vision created by your imagination and project this beautiful picture of yours onto outside circumstances. When you master your intellectual faculty of perception you live in freedom and you create.

Your perception is your projection of the world. Use this fact for your highest good. The eyes are useless if the mind is blind.

Sapere Vedere — Knowing How to See

No one has ever expressed this statement better than Leonardo da Vinci. He had a personal motto defined in the simplicity of two words: *sapere vedere*. The phrase is a combination of the Latin word *"sapere,"* which means knowing, and *"vedere,"* which means to see, says Kevin Hall in his book *Aspire*. When we focus our sight on what is life-giving and uplifting in our circumstances, ourselves, and others, we truly know how to see. When we start looking at things with understanding rather than just seeing with our simple receptive sight sensors, we express our higher selves as spiritual beings. Da Vinci understood that we see with our eyes, and with our mind, but we also know how to "see" with our hearts. When we use our hearts (our genuine passion and desires), we can create a vision for our lives.

Your Perception

When you have a vision, you become the master of your life. You are free from any circumstance.

I was deeply impressed by a greeting in the movie *Avatar*. The citizens of the village placed a hand on the other person's heart, looked into their eyes, and said, "I see you." They did not say hello or good morning, but "I see you."

What if everybody else could see you in your greatness, your true essence? What if you could see others in their greatness? The world would certainly be a different place. Communication between people would change, as there would be no competition, resistance, fights, criticism, or religious or political differences. Only freedom and creation.

I would like to leave you with a poem that I wrote:

> I see YOU
> and because I see YOU
> I have no worries
> I feel no pain
> I have no doubts
> And I pray
> If only you could see me.

Live your life and always bring forth more of you; move forward, be big, have faith, develop your mind's eye. Enjoy the happiness of today, fill it with your presence, and create yourself and your world.

Victoria Lazarova, Bulgaria

Chapter 6

Your Intuition

The key to experience freedom from struggle.

By Dawn R. Nocera

"Prayer is when you talk to God; intuition is when God talks to you."

~ Dr. Wayne Dyer

"*D*id you see that crash!?"

It was the middle of the night and my brother and I both stepped out of our rooms and faced each other, dumbfounded. We had both been wakened in the middle of the night and looked out each of our bedroom windows just in time to see a car crash and break the telephone pole in front of our house. We saw the driver get out and run away.

That night, my brother and I searched the street for signs of a crash before he hit the pole, like skid marks on the road, or another car that might have been hit before that car hit the pole. We found no signs. We walked up and down the street looking for an explanation for why we both woke up before the crash. We found nothing. The police officers found no reason that we would wake up before the crash, either, and they did not believe us.

Intuition is like that. It hits you, you act, and if you try to explain the workings of intuition to someone else, you are likely to get a lot of backlash. "There is no way it happened like that!" "You couldn't have known that!" "Someone must have told you!"

In everyday life, intuition is a little more subtle. It comes to you in a flash of insight about how to finish a project, or knowledge about someone else that comes without reason. It may or may not wake you up in the middle of the night.

Perhaps you are one of those people who doubt that your intuition exists. Maybe you have a lot of intuition about many things and you haven't quite figured out how to use that intuition productively. The challenge for most people is trusting their intuition. I have yet to meet a person who has not had a moment of intuitive insight, and yet most people have little knowledge to help them understand what intuition is or how they can develop trust in themselves to use their intuition in a way that creates the much-sought-after freedom from struggle and in turn aids them in living their fullest self-expression.

This chapter will help you understand what your intuition is and help you gain trust in your ability to harness your intuition, act on it, and move forward in life with ease and joy, free from struggle.

Intuition is Your Natural State of Being

Our lives were meant to be easy. We were meant to live our lives as natural expressions of our higher selves. We were meant to connect deeply with the very spirit of life itself and tune into our inner wisdom. We were designed to receive guidance as it comes effortlessly from the very source of life through this inner wisdom, and we were designed to be fearless in acting on these ideas and impulses.

When you were an infant, you were very much in tune with your environment. If the people around you were upset, it upset you. You were designed to mirror the attitude of those around you to keep you safe. Around the age of seven, you began to develop your own ideas and attitudes. You began to develop your free will. In a loving environment that is designed for your ultimate self-expression and growth, and you would have tested your new ideas and begun to create a definite belief system about life. In a perfect environment, you would be free to evolve and create new understandings that are either in harmony with the beliefs of your family or that create beliefs and ideas that are independent of your family. Either way, you would come to know yourself deeply and be understanding of the choices others make through their experiences. Ideally, you would remain in tune with your higher self and the impulses of wisdom that are relayed to you through your subconscious mind by your emotions — and you would naturally grow into your fullest self-expression.

Making use of your intuition guides you to know your life purpose, have perfect vision for your future, and to live with ease and joy. Using your intuition is a habit of freeing yourself from struggle as you create the life you want.

Intuition Then and Now

In the past, oracles, seers and medicine people of Eastern cultures wrote much of what has been written on intuition. According to an article by Dr. Sarvepalli Radhakrishnan, in Hindu and Buddhist thought, intuition was associated with the highest of the spiritual states that could only be achieved through meditation or mental discipline. Even though many Western thinkers, such as Pythagoras, Plato, Aristotle, and others, taught that knowledge exists without proof and could be accessed through intuition, the Western world put intuition aside as a practice or as an education for future generations, and chose instead to practice the science of physical cause and effect. The basic building blocks of science ask the question, "What is your hypothesis?" The idea of guessing what will happen in a scientific experiment is sometimes confused with intuition. Guessing in this way is usually a function of the reasoning faculty, where a guess is formed from previous knowledge. It is not a sudden flash of insight and certainly not intuition. Move up the ladder of achievement in science, or any other field of performance and study, and you find minds filled with wonder, curiosity and exploration. It is from this place intuition is sparked.

> "The intuitive mind is a sacred gift and the rational mind is a faithful servant. We have created a society that honors the servant and has forgotten the gift." ~ Albert Einstein

Today, we truly are living in an amazing time, where philosophers, psychologists, and healers use science to not only prove the existence of intuition, but also to really explain it in a way that we can begin to trust it as a natural part of our design and teach new generations how to direct, trust, and act on their intuition in daily life to make changes that move the world forward, reaching for more life, exploring new ideas, and creating things that were once thought impossible.

After reading this chapter, you will gain knowledge and clarity about how you can direct your intuition. This new understanding will give you confidence and trust; however, only you will be able to take action on what your intuition tells you. Action is the razor's edge that is the finest line between success and failure. You get to decide what you are going to do or not do. Your intuition is there to guide you.

Intuition as Gateway to Discovery

I love studying the life of Albert Einstein. The more I study his writings, the more I understand intuition and see that it truly is the gateway to discovery. Let's look at his quote again: "The intuitive mind is a sacred gift and the rational mind is a faithful servant. We have created a society that honors the servant and has forgotten the gift."

What exactly does this mean, and why do scientists really "get" this intuition? I have studied success for more than 20 years in all areas. I have worked with many successful business owners, professional athletes, inventors, and top-performing salespeople. Across the board, intuition is one of many ideas that help people move themselves and society forward into growth and possibility. People who can let go of the need to see things on paper and jump into an idea that they have no basis for understanding in reality are the people who create new ideas and are rewarded by seeing their ideas come to life in their physical reality. They are the people who move the world forward. Albert Einstein was not the first person to talk about the intuitive mind and how it helped him see opportunities where other people saw problems, so he was free to manifest new discoveries in life.

He was convinced that intuition is really the key to understanding this basic creative force of the universe. Albert Einstein said, "I believe energy is the basic force in all creation," and when we realize that intuition is just that ability to tune into or read the energies of all of creation, of all the world, then you might understand why he was excited about using his intuition — and not just excited, because he used it as if it was his only tool! Beyond that, he had people who worked with him that saw to it that the math matched the intuition. Most people are afraid to trust their intuition in this way.

I want to help you to step into trust. I would like to invite you to take a close look at your life and say, "Is there any area of my life where I can use my intuition to move forward, and let go of some of my old ideas and outdated thinking about how the world works?" Then step up and step into a new role. Take some time to read about Einstein's life. You will see that his whole life was surrounded by the idea of the role intuition played in scientific discovery. He also said, "The only real valuable thing is intuition. This is the value of life." I believe when he said, "I only want to know the thoughts of God. All else are details," he was providing us with a direction to go to discover our own answers. If you are going to tap into intuition, why not go for the creative source, which is that creative idea, to really tap into the truth? It is the divine, and what the divine knows about you is the truth, and that is what Einstein is inviting us to do.

Go back and become like a child. We are naturally very intuitive. I have three children and I remember when they were little. If I quietly entered their bedrooms when they were sleeping they would wake up. They could intuitively feel my presence around them. That is how you are born, and that is how you are designed to live. You are designed to sense and feel the energy of your environment without someone telling you how to feel or how to think. As a child you were confident and you trusted yourself. As we grow older, we can take actions to make changes in the environment if what we feel doesn't match what we want to feel. That is key, and I am going to repeat it: we can use our physical body to move our environment, to make the changes that we want, as well as see it in our mind's eye. We can also change our physical environment to create a different vibration. Clean up your environment. However, if we do not clean up the image we hold in our mind of our environment, things will return to the way they were.

What is Intuition?

"The ability to understand something instinctively, without the need for conscious reasoning, a thing that one knows or considers likely from instinctive feeling rather than conscious reasoning." ~ Oxford Dictionaries

"The act or faculty of knowing or sensing without the use of rational processes; immediate cognition."~ The Free Dictionary

Intuition is our ability to tune into the energy that surrounds us. It is our ability to tune into the people around our environments, a situation, an event, or us. It is our ability to hear what is going on behind spoken words. It is our ability to connect deeply with our environment. Intuition allows you to have knowledge, without the understanding of how you know it.

Dr. Wayne Dyer explains, "For the spiritual being, intuition is far more than a hunch. It is viewed as guidance or as God talking, and this inner insight is never taken lightly or ignored." He also said, "Prayer is when you talk to God; intuition is when God talks to you."

Napoleon Hill calls intuition your sixth sense. Hill says that the sixth sense is the "receiving set" through which ideas, plans, and thoughts flash into the mind. These flashes are sometimes called "hunches" or "inspirations.'" He also said that it is a mixture of both the mental and spiritual, and the medium of contact between the finite mind of man and Infinite Intelligence.

The Law of Vibration

To really understand intuition, you need to understand the Law of Vibration and the Law of Attraction. The Law of Vibration tells us that everything moves. Every cell of your body, every molecule that makes up the chair you sit in or the car you drive is in a constant state of motion. You move and produce energy all the time, even as you sleep. After your last breath of life your physical body continues to be in motion. This type of motion is called decomposition or disintegration. The motion of growth and life expanding is called creation. Bob Proctor often says, "You are either creating or disintegrating. That is all there is to it." As each one of your cells vibrates and moves, whether you are alive or not, it gives off energy. The energy that your body gives off is your attitude. It is something you cannot hide. People pick up on it, consciously and unconsciously.

If you and I are talking to each other, I would be able to tune into your vibration or your attitude, and I would become better able to serve you. If your vibration or attitude rises, I will feel it — that is, if I am tuned in. We will get to "how to tune in" later in the chapter. You may find it interesting that our willingness to work together creates an entirely new combined vibration. My energy and your energy combined creates a new and stronger energy field. Groups of people working or living together create a similar social attitude. When they can attach their attitude and values to a collective goal, like we did to write this book, their energy combines as a single unit of energy. It is like a battery: the more cells, the more powerful!

Imagine you have a goal to own a new home, and you walk into a beautiful home for sale, and you immediately pick up a strong sense of negativity. The home is perfect for you and your family, though you just can't seem to shake the idea that something is wrong. Your intuition is reading the home's energy, and it is doing it without your request. It is an automatic function of our intellect. Your intuition gives you the ability to feel the energy within you and feel the energy around you. Intuition is our awareness of pure energy that is the essence of everything we encounter.

Intuition aligns your will and divine will, activating confidence to change the course of the world. Intuition allows you to see what others may miss in the present. Intuition allows you to tune in to your present environment. This is vital to understand when you are working toward your own personal growth or toward a focused goal. Your intuition illuminates the opportunities for you to move forward with greater ease. Without the use of your intuition you would not recognize opportunities as they come.

Why You May Want to Use Your Intuition

> "Intuition cuts down on time and effort. As you gain intuitive intelligence you become more energy and time effective." ~ Doc Childre

When you regain access to your natural state of growth, you let go of struggle and life becomes very easy. You achieve goals more quickly. The opportunities come faster and with fewer barriers. If there has ever been a time for you to stop struggling and letting go of the need to make things difficult, it is now, because time is important. You have a lot of good work to do on this Earth. You were put here for some very special reason. Everybody on Earth was put here for a higher purpose, and our belief that things are difficult extends the time needed for the achievement of our goals. I would like to encourage you to let go of the idea of struggle and frustration so you can achieve your goals faster. You may understand at some level that struggling to accomplish a task slows down the process. It does not make it faster. You think you are working harder to help the goal arrive faster and it is entirely the opposite. Tune into your intuition and it will show you which direction to go to find your easy and effortless path, and with practice you will come to understand that this is how it was meant to be. You were meant to check with your inner wisdom first and then take a step in the direction offered by your intuition. You were not meant to ask around and see what other people think before you decide to step in that direction. If you do the opportunity may no longer be there. It is natural to seek out easier ways to do things and you should understand that letting go of the struggle makes things happen really quick!

Another reason you will want to use your intuition is that it allows you to see what others miss. When you let go of the struggle, your peripheral vision expands. Oxygen flows to the cells of your brain and your body, and your eyes get to see more. Your physical eyes in actuality get to see peripherally, where before you may have had tunnel vision. I am not just talking spiritually, I am talking about driving down the road, and seeing more in your view. Intuition allows you to align your desires with your actions. The biggest, most unbelievable, life-changing opportunities could be in front of you at this very moment and you might not be able to see them. Intuition triggers that confidence to change the course of the world, and at the same time it provides the serenity you need to stay the course. It activates confidence and provides serenity and peace of mind.

How I Began Using my Intuition

I often say, "There is an easy and effortless path to success, and unfortunately few are brave enough to travel it!" If it were true, that there is an easy and effortless path to success and authentic abundance, why then would you have to be brave to travel it?

When I started down my journey of learning to trust my intuition, which is what you want to do if you want to travel that easy and effortless path, I thought that it would lead me to do things I did not want to do. I thought for sure I would be led to long, miserable hours of work, sacrificing my dreams, and painful servitude. Most of all, I thought that really following my intuition would mean I would have to give up my dreams and sacrifice everything I ever wanted to serve some higher cause. I thought for sure that my life would get very hard and, as difficult as it is for me to admit it, I was scared.

I wanted evidence. I needed proof that I could make sense of that and following my intuition was going to help me achieve the kind of success I wanted in my life.

At the time, I was deep in the study of what separates successful people from the masses, and the more I immersed myself in the study of success and peak performance, the more I realized that if I wanted to be more, do more, and have more, I had to trust more. Every success story I read had an account of someone trusting their gut, going with their own ideas despite all the odds against them, and in the end winning because they followed their intuition instead of following reason, logic or the caution given by their well-meaning friends and family.

Oprah Winfrey tells how she felt when she read the book, *The Color Purple*. She connected with the character Sofia and just knew she had to play the role. At the time, she had not been in any movies, had no ties to the industry, and no evidence, reason or logic backing the idea that she would someday play Sofia when they turned the book into a movie. Despite a few false hopes, she eventually received the call she knew would come where Steven Spielberg asked her to audition for the role. She trusted her intuition.

Alejandro Torres-Marco, author of the chapter on your reasoning faculty, told me about a dream he had when his daughter was about two years old, and in the dream, her room was on fire. He immediately woke up and went to check on her to find her with a very high fever and sought proper care.

In both cases, trusting their intuition seemed to give them unwavering self-confidence and faith in their decisions. The intuition was there, and their decision to listen and act upon it shaped their lives just as it does ours.

Following my intuition has led me down the most joyful and

carefree path I could ever imagine. Where in the past I tried to focus my attention and energy on what I wanted and worked hard to stay on the hamster wheel getting very little results, I now notice the ease that accompanies all areas of my life. Now when I listen to my intuition, take action, and follow up by creating a plan using my reasoning faculty, life is not hard at all — it really is easy and effortless. The more I follow my intuition, the easier life becomes. When I feel as if I am struggling, I slowly say out loud, "Easy and effortless, easy and effortless, that is how I like it. Easy and effortless." The best part is that I have accomplished so much in such a short period of time. For me, learning to relax and trust myself puts me in a sort of "time warp" where things move quickly and with ease. My intuition led me to write this book with my amazing co-authors. I have traveled more for pleasure than I have in my entire life since deliberately taking this path. I have connected more deeply with my family and made new and meaningful friendships. My ability to act on my intuition has really changed everything. Some call it bliss, and an athlete might say I am living in "the zone". It doesn't mean that I don't get frustrated, I do. It doesn't mean that I don't have to work at all, I do. What it does mean is that I have the confidence that what I am doing is right. The frustration I feel is a blessing; it helps me remember that life does not have to be that hard. And when I do get frustrated, I tune into the energy of ease and flow and ask, "What do I need to do, remember, or see that would make this easier?"

In the beginning, and long before being awakened in the middle of the night to see the car crash into the pole in front of our house, I randomly tuned into my intuition; however, I did not know how to tune my intuition into the energy I wanted to tune into. I would pick up the energy of a street corner and feel nauseated. I would pick up the energy of sick people in my classes in college and feel horrible for no reason. I did not know how to focus my intuition or how to shield myself from the negative energy that surrounded me. I was very open and receptive, but I did not know how to train my subconscious to tune into the vibes I wanted to tune into.

I once had a dream about an old friend's sister being pregnant. There was nothing significant about the dream, only that she was pregnant. I hadn't talked to this friend in a long time, so I thought telling him about my dream would be a great reason to call and catch up. However when I told him about my dream, he assured me that his sister was not pregnant, and he went on to tell me how ridiculous the dream was. "She is married and finishing up nursing school," he said. "Having a baby would ruin everything she has worked so hard for!" He was actually angry at the thought of my dream. I wrote that dream off as a subconscious effort to connect with him and nothing more until a week later when he called me to tell me the news, his sister was pregnant and she found out the day I called him.

I had a runaway intuition. I would receive information all the time about people, places and events that I really had no business knowing about and certainly no inclination to share with anyone else. The bits of insight I received were not always welcome, like the dream I shared with my friend about his sister. I had no reason directing my intuition. When I finally began to explore my intuition and direct it, that is when life really changed for me.

Learning to trust my intuition has been a journey. Learning to direct my intuition toward definite ends has given me the most tangible rewards. Learning to be patient with myself along the way has been the greatest gift to myself, and I am still learning this one!

Your intuition may be running wild, as well. You may be so busy picking up ideas for other people that you do not recognize when those messages are meant for you. Maybe you are the guy who receives great insight at the last minute and doesn't act on it, then feels like a victim when someone else gets the same idea, acts on it, and gets the credit for "your" idea. In reality, all ideas are simply energy. They are there for you to act on, and those who do are the ones that gain the benefits of their actions. If you take anything from this chapter, please make note of this: intuition will not pay the bills, but acting on your intuition can bring you rich rewards! The action is what sets in motion the attraction.

Intuition or Paradigms

As I tried to use my intuition more and more, I realized that I was very intuitive. I picked up energy all the time. I wanted to use this tool to help my own growth, not just to randomly pick up energy from strangers. There was one problem: I did not trust my intuition. I did not trust my feelings. I began to act on many thoughts that I labeled "intuition" and nothing magical happened, nothing changed! I was not growing. I was not achieving my goals. I was stuck. I wasn't aware that we receive information from our intuition and from our previous programming (our paradigms). I was mistaking paradigms for intuition, and my paradigms did not prove to be the best guide. Listening to my paradigms always led me right back to the place I started from, stuck in a comfort zone. Let me explain.

When we were facilitating training on *7 Keys to Freedom*, someone asked this question: "I am thinking about my new goal, but these crazy thoughts keep coming up in my mind. How can I tell the difference between thoughts coming from intuition, thoughts coming from spirit, and thoughts that are coming from my paradigms? How can one tell the difference?"

This is a great question. We are designed to listen and follow our intuition; however, most of us relive our paradigms and feel stuck, very stuck. Becoming an expert in distinguishing intuition from paradigms will be fun once you understand the subtle differences, and you commit to following one and not the other.

You may have already taken hold of the idea that intuition moves you forward and moves you toward growth, expansion and more life, while paradigms keep you moving in circles. Paradigms have been discussed throughout this book, and for a very good reason: the only obstacle there is to your success in any area of life is a paradigm, or habit, that no longer serves you. Following your intuition is the easiest way to make a quantum leap in the results you get. However, intuition does not have a face; you cannot prove your intuitive ideas to your colleagues and friends. Most of the time, you can only make up reasons to back your intuition, while not disclosing the fact that you are moving forward based on your gut feeling. You see, both intuition and paradigms show up in your life by means of your emotions. If you pay close attention, you will find that a feeling coming from a paradigm is a reaction to something outside of yourself. Intuition, on the other hand, requires you to respond to a situation, and often does not show up unless asked. Intuition is nonjudgmental. It may ask you to do something that you do not believe you are capable of doing. It may ask you to speak to someone you have been avoiding. Intuition does not judge your ability or anything about anyone involved. On the other hand, paradigms are judgmental. If an idea is a paradigm, it comes with preconceived notions about other people, places, or events. Paradigms bring with them a core of fear, doubt and worry. Intuition brings with it love, understanding, and an open mind. There is no doubt with intuition: you just know.

Daniel Kahneman, who is widely regarded as one of the modern world's most influential psychologists, points out that intuition is a system of thinking that happens automatically and naturally. He labels this system of thinking simply, "System 1" and labels the second basic system, which is our reason, "System 2."

System 1 is fast. System 2 is slow. System 1 is void of doubt or fear. It is quick, automatic, and, according to Kahneman, not always accurate. System 2, which operates out of reason, gathers information that is stored in our subconscious mind to make a decision. System 2 is run on past knowledge, unconscious beliefs, and previous understanding, while System 1 runs on inspiration. The table below outlines both systems. This is good to know, because we need both systems to operate effectively; otherwise, we may become reckless in our actions or the opposite, paralyzed with fear into a state of inaction.

System 1 - Intuition	System 2 - Reason
✓ Quick ✓ Automatic and natural thinking ✓ Void of doubt or fear ✓ Runs on inspiration ✓ Not always accurate	✓ Slow ✓ Gathers information that is stored in our subconscious mind to make a decision ✓ Runs on past knowledge, unconscious beliefs, and previous understanding

Reason and paradigms are not the same. A paradigm is subconscious programming. It is already there, and your reason gives you the ability to think the way you want to think about any idea. If intuition is our guide to our fullest self-expression, our reason is the tool we need to use to discover whether the idea that came to us is an intuitive insight or an old idea or paradigm reappearing to keep us safe and on a hamster wheel.

Most of us seek out reason first and discount our body's natural success system. We haven't taken the time to get to know how it works and how to discern which system we are working with. The natural process would be to listen to your intuition and then follow it up with reason. This is our natural path of growth and fulfillment. We are designed to learn and grow, trust our intuitions, and act on it using reason. When systems 1 and 2 work in harmony, we call it wisdom. If you only listen to System 1, it would be called reckless, and if you only listen to System 2, or your reasoning faculty, you would find yourself doing many of the same things you have always done and getting the same results. When both reason and intuition work together, life moves forward effortlessly.

To recognize the kind of feeling that indicates true guidance, look for three qualities: calmness, clarity and joy. Intuition is always based in a deep sense of calmness and detachment.

The best way to learn the difference is to pay attention to your feelings and practice! I get better and better every day at using and trusting my intuition, and it serves me well — and this took time.

If you are looking for evidence that your intuition is activated, here are some signs:

When You Use Your Intuition	When Your Paradigms Are in Control
✓ You feel at peace with the decision. ✓ Your decisions are based on what you want. ✓ You feel a sense of freedom.	✓ You feel panic around the decision. ✓ You react or make decisions out of fear. ✓ You feel trapped.

How to Recognize and Trust Your Intuition

If you remember, Dr. Kahneman said that intuition comes quickly and comes without doubt, fear, or anxiety. Some people get a sudden flash of insight that comes with confidence and faith, and they immediately attempt to connect that insight to their conditioned experiences of how the world works. So instead of cultivating the faith and trusting their intuition, they begin to doubt what their intuition has shown them — and that doubt turns into fear and fear turns into anxiety. It seems reasonable that trusting your intuition would be a sure way to end anxiety.

Even in life or death situations, when your intuition takes over there is a sense of calm and deliberate action that comes from being totally aware of what needs to be done to save a life or to escape harm. Many of the nurses and professionals in the medical field who shared their stories with Elizabeth Lloyd Mayer, while she was doing the research for her book, *Extraordinary Knowing*, reported that in crisis situations they just knew what to do. This is the Law of Life taking over. The Law of Life says, "More life to all!"

Becoming a master of your feelings and emotions is necessary for mastering your intuition. If you have runaway emotions, it is hard to distinguish any intuitive flashes. Learning to calm your emotions, not suppress them but calm them, leads to mastery of self and the ability to tune into your environment.

You can also use your feelings to gauge where you are regarding what you want out of life. If you are feeling frustrated and overwhelmed, chances are you simply need to use your intellectual faculties to change your perspective, focus, and find a better feeling. Once you feel good and you direct your thoughts, instead of suppressing them, you can be certain that you are aligned with what you want — and that understanding leads you to release any worry or doubt that you have about your life.

Most people have been trained to turn off emotions so they don't upset other people; however, the only way we can find the self-mastery we seek is to tune into our own feelings and direct them with our will toward what we want in our lives.

The most successful people make the effort to develop their intuition. They know that their feelings are like a radar device that tunes into universal knowledge and Infinite Intelligence. They understand that the source of their feelings is spirit within them.

How to Develop and Trust your Intuition

The first thing I say to people, especially if you are a little bit intuitive, is to find yourself a goal, a desire. The thing that you desire the most is the carrot on the stick in front of the horse. It is the activator to move you forward. Seek your goals and when you focus your energy and attention on what it is you want then you begin to attract solely the ideas and energy that are aligned with your goal and your desire. That is exciting, because you become a "quick" magnet to attract the things you need to hit your goal, to achieve, to become, to allow. Tapping into your intuition is more about allowing yourself to be who you were meant to be than it is about achieving a goal. However, the goal of your desire is to get you to move forward; to get you to move in the direction of your higher purpose. I hope this makes sense for you, so you can use this in your own life.

Intuition is very closely linked to the Law of Polarity, which says everything has an equal and an opposite. Up has a down, in has an out, left has a right, and so on. You can tune in just as easily to the good of the situation as you can tune into the bad. I really want you to understand this concept. There are people who are tuned into only the negative energy of the world around them, and this is what they attract. However, the fact that you are reading this book tells me that you want freedom from this negativity. You really want to tune in to what is good. So when you practice using your intuition, really practice being in tune to the good, because it will get you into the habit of practicing and seeing what is amazing and wonderful in the world.

I invite you to trust. Trust is something you will have to work on and do on your own. Trust that using your intuition can create massive change in your life for the good. How quickly you tap into your intuition determines how quickly you make a quantum leap. Everybody wants the kind of quantum leap that makes an impact on the world. You can make leaps without using your intuition. However, your intuition is the one thing that will help you make the quantum leap that you really want at your core level.

The Master Key to Unlock Intuition

What is the master key that unlocks your intuition? You may have already guessed it. The master key is the "question"! We are constantly given answers to all of our questions. Remember the saying, "Ask and it is given?" That is the way we are designed. We are created to ask and receive. We are always being answered, but most of us ask the wrong questions. We ask, "Why are things hard?" or "Why are things so difficult?" Instead, we should be asking, "Why are things easy?" "How can this be easier?" You are going to want to become a master at asking yourself the right questions.

So, the master key is the question you ask. If you are a salesperson ready to make a sales call, instead of picking up the list that you made yesterday, you might ask your master key question, "Who do I need to call today?" You listen to whatever your intuitive mind gives you, and you do it. While the key to intuition is the question, action is required for you to receive the results. So my call to action for you is, whom are you really listening to? Are you listening to your outside world? Are you listening to your environment? Are you listening to your old paradigms? Or are you listening to your heart? Are you tapping into the desire that is in your heart? Your desire comes from your heart. Are you listening to your heart?

Affirmations Can Help

Here are some affirmations you can use to help you tap into your intuition:

"I easily and effortlessly attract all the information, people, and events that aid in my service to the world." After all, that's what it's all about. It is about you giving service to the world. The universe will reward you.

"I easily and effortlessly align with the truth in all situations." Intuition is the ability to tap into the truth in every single situation. Tapping into the underlying truth, we are all united and connected.

"I easily and effortlessly focus on where I am going, and the way will be shown."

These are some excellent affirmations to help you move forward.

A Summary

You are born with intuition; everyone has it and, according to Sonia Choquette, there are four steps that you can use to develop your intuition.

The first step is to be open to it! Allow yourself to play with the idea that you have access to powerful sources of unseen wisdom that you can call on at will. The second step is to expect it. Expect that you will receive an answer to your questions. The third step is to trust it. Trust that your intuition is there to guide you toward your goals and toward more life. Write those intuitive hunches down when they come to you, or at least speak them out loud. The fourth step is to allow yourself to experiment with your intuition and act on it. Take action on your intuition immediately. Remember that the universe loves speed. You don't have to know why you are doing anything, and it is often better that you don't know all the details when you act on intuition. Intuition will always take you where you need to be.

There is magic in taking that first step, and then the universe shows you the next step. Most people will get off track when using their intuition. They think they are picking up on the energy of the goal, when in fact they are picking up on the energy of the paradigm, yours and everyone else's!

1. Be clear on your goal or desire. What do you want?

2. Be open to receiving intuition that will guide you in that direction.

3. Expect your intuition to show you the opportunities as they come.

4. Trust that your intuition will indeed move you forward.

5. And act! Act on your intuitive hunches as quickly as possible.

Intuition comes to you in many ways, through dreams, through hunches, through visions. Sometimes it comes and you have instant clarity about a situation, and other times you may only pick up a piece of information that doesn't make sense to you until years later, when you look back on how all the pieces fit together. The highest purpose of your intuition is to allow you to see the opportunities that you might otherwise dismiss. When you act on the opportunities as they come to you and know that your path is being illuminated by Infinite Intelligence, it is easier to be confident in taking action. Intuition is not only a key to help you find freedom from struggle; it is also a key to ultimate self-discovery.

Dawn R. Nocera, USA

Chapter 7

Your Will

The key to manifesting freedom.

By Dawn R. Nocera and SEVEN

"Use your willpower to keep your mind off the subject of poverty, and to keep it fixed with faith and purpose on the vision of what you want."

~ Wallace Wattles

When my son was growing up, it seemed like getting him to do anything I asked was a struggle. It didn't matter if I asked him to brush his teeth, or if I asked him to clean up his room. His favorite response was, "I will." And each time he answered saying, "I will," I questioned, "When?" This happened regularly. Our emotions rose and my patience plummeted. We went around in circles like this until one day, right in the middle of the battle of "I wills," it occurred to me how ridiculous it really was. While both of us held our ground, what needed to be done was left undone. It is interesting how we use the word "will" without actually using our will.

Your will is your most important asset. Like my son, most of us say we will do something, but fall short of actually doing it.

Think of the area of your life that you really want to change, or improve. I have found that most people know what they need to do to create that change, but they just don't do it. They do not do what is needed to be done a lot of times simply because they do not understand how to apply their will in a way that creates easy and effortless manifestation of their desires. They get stuck in a belief that it will be hard or it will take too much time.

There is a way to apply your will so the action that you take comes naturally and without struggle. Unfortunately, we use our will to create more of the same in our life and think we have to use our will to force us to do something we don't want to do, like my son and cleaning his room. We think we have to summon up our will to force us to do something we don't want to do. To force something is to say, "I am not willing to do it, but I will force myself to anyway." Force is just that, *force*. It is pressure. Force is just as real on the mental plane as it is on the physical plane between two objects. Force negates everything. For every action, there is an equal and opposite reaction. When we use our will to force ourselves to do anything, people call it "willpower." Though many people have been very successful using their will in this way, you will discover by reading this chapter that power is not the highest use of the will.

Your will is an intellectual faculty and, when used properly, it creates lasting change in your programming, not just temporary change in action. Your will is not a force, and it is not a result. Your will is the faculty that allows you to change outcomes, not just create more of the same. This change happens inside of you, and it is as thin as a razor's edge.

Will and Work

It is a common expression to say, "I have to do this," or "I have to do that." The word "have" implies the forced obligation to do something by some outside force. If you stop and think about it, you never "have" to do anything. When you understand that it is your choice to do what you do, you will not "have to" anymore. You become conscious of the decision you are making by your action. When you say, "I have to go to work," you really don't "have to," do you? Every day you make a decision to go to work as opposed to staying home or doing something else, because of the benefits you receive through the work you do. I hope this understanding helps you see your work from a different perspective. By transforming the thought, "I have to go to work," to "I choose to go to work," you put the responsibility of the work that you do where it belongs, with you! With this new perspective, you become aware of how to use your will, not to force you to do something you don't want to do, but to change your perspective of the work you do. Find its benefit first, and then doing the work will seem easier and less stressful than ever before.

For you to use your will in a way that creates lasting change in your life, look at your will in a new light. See your will for what it really is: your ability to take responsibility and transform the energy of your faculties.

Turn Fear into Faith

Your will's most appropriate use is simply to turn fear into faith. Think of a successful marathon runner for a moment. She does not force herself past the "runner's wall." What she does is take the energy, the fear that she cannot make it past the finish line, and she transforms that energy into faith that she can. She chooses to finish! Using your will in the way it was intended always results in faith; anything else is force, and I want to remind you that force always negates. Force creates an equal and opposite force that pushes back. Force creates resistance to the very change you are attempting to create! However when you use your will in the way it was intended, you transform the energy of stagnation into the energy of creation, and the energy of stuck into the energy of luck. You actually release your resistance to the success you want, and allow yourself to be a part of the energy of life itself. You become responsible for your own success.

The Highest Use of Your Will

You now know the difference between using your will as force and using your will to create faith. Let me explain what your will is so you can use it to create the change you really want in any area of your life. The highest use of your will is to keep your intellectual faculties in the position that enables you to maintain the clearest vision of yourself experiencing the best possible outcome that you can imagine. This clarity of vision inspires the most efficient, purposeful, and natural action possible. When you use your will as it was intended, your growth and self-expression become a natural part of life, and you no longer have the need to fight with yourself in order to overcome some perceived obstacle or challenge. Within the clear vision of the best possible outcome, there is no room for doubt or opposing forces. You hold the vision and realize that your success or failure is a choice.

Read the above paragraph again. In it is everything you need to change every aspect of your life. Your will shifts your internal frequency of vibration from one level to another. Imagine using your will to stop fighting with yourself over how you look or the amount of food you eat. What would it be like for you to have a relationship with your body that supported your purpose in life instead of using your body as an excuse why you "can't" live your life's purpose?

Single-Minded Focus

Focusing on what you want as opposed to what you don't want is essential for changing your energy from fear to faith, and it can happen with relative ease if you have an ounce of focusing power. Change the idea that you have to force yourself to lose weight because you are afraid that people won't like you or even worse, you won't like yourself if you are not thin. Focus on the health and fitness you already have by the very fact that you are alive. Think about the organs in your body that do function well. Instead of taking your health for granted, really take some time to appreciate your physical body and all of its automatic functions. Your heart beats, your lungs breathe, your neurons fire, all without your direction or attention. Allow the idea that your health can increase into your mind. This shift is probably the single most important act you can do for yourself. It creates faith in yourself and your abilities. That tiny seed of faith is usually all it takes to move from knowing what to do, to doing it. Focus is the real power behind your will. What you focus on, though, is always a choice.

Much of what has been written about the will talks about concentration. Concentration is the mental effort of focusing one's attention. I would like to invite you to pay attention to the difference in your own emotions when you think of focus and concentration. The feeling should not be a feeling of struggle or weariness; you will want to find a feeling of freedom or relief.

Your will is the tool that bridges the mental and spiritual worlds and the material world. It is the intellectual faculty that transforms thoughts and ideas into things and experiences in your life. When you are focused on your desire and feel yourself in possession of that desire, your focus and attention is where it should be and all action taken from this place aligns with the easiest and most joyful experience possible in attaining that desire. Remember, where you focus your attention is your choice.

Think back on your life to a time when you had extreme focus on a single outcome. For some it may remind you of when you single-mindedly pursued that first date, first job or college graduation. Each time you had extreme focus in your life you had a goal in mind. There was an outcome or a result that you wanted to achieve. There was some aim or direction that guided you to think, feel, and act a certain way.

Your first transformation will come from changing the idea of force into the idea of clarity and focus. Your focus will shift to your desire or the goal you want to achieve and away from what you don't want. You will begin to really feel free and that freedom is the transformation you seek. Remember, your feelings are your ultimate tool to guide you toward your desire.

> **MEMORY Journaling Exercise:**
>
> Take a moment to think back on your life and remember those times that you had clear focus. Write them down as they come to you. This will activate your faith in yourself and give you an idea of how you have used your will appropriately in the past.

Willing to Succeed, by Alejandro Marco-Torres

For me, will is undoubtedly the cause of accomplishment. I was 22 and had just finished my college studies in biology. Since one of my passions is scuba diving, I wanted to be at the highest status that a diver could be, so I decided to study commercial diving. I was determined to become one no matter what. But first, I had to persuade my father to give me permission and economic support to do so. Being the sixth of nine children, and the first one to dare to ask for it, you can imagine this was not an easy first step. Fortunately, at that time, my family's finances were in good shape, and with my added promise that I would pay back the whole expense to accomplish my dream, I went to The Commercial Diving Center in California, USA.

I was one happy man!

Once I started my studies, I found out that the student who graduated first of his class could win a working contract grant with an offshore oil underwater construction company. This grant became my new goal that would test my will and determination. Then, I was not aware of the value of my mind faculties and how important the will is. Nevertheless, I was determined to win it. I was one hundred percent focused. I had extreme focus. Since I was a foreigner and a rookie, I knew I faced some challenges in getting a job with an international underwater corporation. I knew I would need every possible advantage. After a few months of doing my best and competing against more than 25 students from all around the world, I accomplished the goal. I finished first in my class. Did I get the coveted job, the one I desired and focused my will on? No, I did not. I found out that there were certain policies within their hiring conditions that prevented it. I felt frustrated at the time, but other than those fleeting feelings, I felt proud. No one could take from me the pride I felt at having accomplished my goal — all thanks to the determination and focus that this great mind faculty gave me.

Are You Willing to Change?

I can hear you now say, "Wow! All I have to do is focus on the health I do have and that will release the extra weight that I have been carrying for years?" Well, that is a start, yet there is another aspect of your will that I would like to introduce you to. If "focus" is one half of your will, then "willingness" is the other half. Your willingness is your will in action. Think of the time when you used your will to achieve the goal you pursued. You focused, and at the same time you did whatever it took. You were willing to fail; you were willing to succeed; you were willing to sacrifice; and you were willing to gain all the rewards that accompanied the result of your focus and attention.

I want you to understand that focusing your attention on what you want is only half the work; the other half comes from your willingness to move in that direction. It is your willingness to take the first step in the direction of your dream. If you cannot see how to reach your goal, take the first step and when you do you will see further. Remember that this is not a forced action; it is a natural direction to travel. When you use your will appropriately you will feel the pull of life moving you into action. My clients have shared with me that once their will was working in the way it was intended, they could not stop themselves from pursuing their desires. Opportunities seemed to pursue them and doors opened for them wherever they went, and it was as if a force of nature summoned them forward. All the actions they took was truly effortless.

Will or a Wall

According to the teacher Michael Beckwith, you will slam into a wall when you keep trying to use your will to force things to turn out the way you want and disregard other factors. He explains in his lectures, be careful not to become so over-focused on what you feel you are entitled to that you lose sight of the big picture, and of your inner needs or the needs of others. Maintain your connection to Infinite Intelligence, which is always concerned with the universal flow of good for all. Become a millionaire, successful, and at the top of your game — and do this while taking care of your health and your relationships with others. Include the best possible outcome in all areas of life while focusing on what you want instead of forcing others to bend to your will, focus on the best possible outcome for everyone involved and remain connected to your higher self.

Can you remember a time when you accomplished things using your will as force, and the results of your efforts resulted in burnout and frustration? At these times, you were not aligned with the best possible outcome for all those involved. You are not alone. We have all experienced this.

Here is Nita Matthews-Morgan's story:

> I remember one time taking a job even though my intuition told me that I was not aligned with all aspects of the work. I wanted the job because it was more money than I had ever made, yet I did not really want to do the tasks the job required. I used my will to go to work at this job and over the next three years, my health began to deteriorate, and I lost

my sense of joy.

I was not using my will, along with my other faculties, to make the situation better, or to leave. I reasoned that if I tried harder, then somehow I could make it work. You can use your will to force yourself to do something, but it takes enormous energy and creates a lot of emotional and physical stress in the process. At the time, I was not aware I could use my faculties to find a better suited place for employment, or that I could use my faculties to help me make the best of the situation. Using your will with each of the other faculties can help you when you decide to stay in a joyless job, as well as help when you decide to find a new place of employment.

According to Price Pritchett, author of You^2, "You do not achieve your dreams, your full potential, through your own singular struggle...neither raw effort nor sheer willpower is the answer. Trying as hard as you can will fall far short of taking you as far as you are capable of going."

Clarity of Vision

You must focus on the images you create with your imagination, of your increased financial abundance, happy relationships, better health, or whatever goal or desire you are pursuing. When you think with the end result in mind you will be guided and encouraged in that direction. You need the focus to keep this picture in your mind. When you are focused and believe that you will have what you desire, there will be no room for thoughts of failure. If thoughts of doubt or failure wrestle with your vision, use your will to return your focus to what you want.

Clarity of vision helps you stay on your natural path of success. Imagine that you have a desire for improved health, and the idea to take a walk comes to you. However, instead of acting on the idea to go for a walk, you decide to force yourself to run, because you have seen others do it to improve their health, and you reason that running is the best and quickest way to improve your health. But instead of finding your health improving, you find you are frustrated by the lack of results as you push yourself more. Sometimes there is a breakdown before you find the easiest way to maintain health, which could be walking not running. There is a natural path to health, and it is there for you to find. If running is the easiest for you, and you find gratification in running, then run. We all have different paths. Our will is there to help us maintain a clear vision that has no room for doubts. This allows us to perceive our natural path to success so we can willingly take the necessary action. It is intended to help us keep our mind clear of doubts, worries and outside influences.

When you have clarity of vision for your goal or the outcome you want, it is easier to see the opportunities that can help you move closer to the goal with ease.

The Purpose of Desire

> "Desire is the effort of the unexpressed possibility within, seeking expression without through your actions."
> ~ Wallace D. Wattles

Your desires come from Infinite Intelligence, and those desires are there to help move you forward. Your higher self is always for more life. Your goal of wanting better health, for example, is there to help you move forward in growth. You may not have known it was Infinite Intelligence giving you this desire. It's your choice the way you choose to meet the goal of better health. You can do it through forced action or inspired will and willingness.

There have been many masters in human history who have given us examples of how to live inspired lives. Besides teaching us to fear nothing, they also taught us not to judge ourselves or other people. Fear comes from judgment, and judgment creates fear. Without judgment there is no fear. Letting go of judgment allows the will to work and allows you to focus, with ease and beauty, and connects you to your higher self and essence, and to your creation. You will especially want to let all thoughts of judgment of yourself go. These thoughts are not from your higher self. They are not inspired will, and they will not lead to inspired actions.

So using the intellectual faculty of your will is really fifty percent focused intention on your goal and fifty percent willingness to do the thing that creates more life so that you are swept up in your desire with ease and flow.

Using Your Will NOW

Your will can only be used in the present. Use your will to bring your faculties in harmony with the present moment. Sometimes people want to use their will to focus on the images of their dreams and their whole energy goes into the future. Then they wonder why they are not able to take any action in the present. Get around that by using your faculties in this moment to do things to move you forward right now. Once you decide what you want, pay attention to your intuition and what it tells you, and as soon as you receive an idea, or a hunch, act on it! Don't wait, do it now. You will be surprised at how quickly your life will transform by using your will not to plan ahead, but to act on the plan you have created with your other faculties. Just like my son, who learned the difference between "I will pick up my room" and actually doing it, so will you!

Using Your Will to Overcome the Odds

According to Thomas Troward, author of *The Edinburgh Lectures on Mental Science*, imagination is the creative function and the will is the centralizing principle. The will's function is to keep the imagination and the other faculties centered in the right direction. The following story illustrates clearly the power of the will.

Nita shared that all her life she used her will to accomplish many things, but one of her most personal stories about the will came after she and her husband decided to adopt a child from Romania:

> In preparation for the adoption, I woke up every day with a huge list of things to do and the determination to do it, all the while holding the vision in my mind of welcoming a new baby into our home. It was incredible that I accomplished this in such a short time. Simply getting a family-child study done of a family to see if they are appropriate

adoptive parents can take months to complete. In six weeks, a group of adoptive parents were flying to Romania with a guide and interpreter. If I didn't get my paperwork done, my husband and I would not be able to go with them. I did it in record time! I have asked myself many times, how did I do that? Looking back, I realize that there was no room for doubt in my mind. The image of flying on a plane to greet a new child was so vivid. This image drove me to quick and efficient action.

Overcoming odds becomes a matter of how well you are able to focus on the task at hand and commit to its completion. Nita used her will to help her stay focused on her vision which assisted in creating efficient effort and streamlined every aspect of her adoption. Her action was infused with purpose. The purpose behind her action created an ease and flow to her actions. The image you hold in the mind can inspire you to continue on and overcome perceived odds. When you are faced with a big challenge in your life, ask yourself, "What image am I holding of the outcome?" How do you perceive the outcome? Are you holding onto the image of the best possible outcome, or the worst-case scenario? Whichever image you hold is directing your path.

As Thomas Troward says, "The will-power, when transferred from the region of the lower mentality to the spiritual plane, becomes simply a calm and peaceful determination to retain a certain mental attitude in spite of all temptations to the contrary, knowing that by doing so the desired result will certainly appear."

Overcoming Indecision

Indecision is one of the worst of all human conditions. It causes many otherwise brilliant people to remain stuck in their careers, relationships and in their present health status. The cause of indecision is simple. Indecision comes from trying to hold two opposing ideas in your mind at the same time. The problem is that it is impossible to keep two thoughts in your mind at the same time. However, many people try to keep several thoughts in their mind at one time. Many of the thoughts we hold onto are opposing ideas. They create a sense of duality in our minds, and these conflicting thoughts remain there until we make a conscious decision to choose one or the other. Without choice, we remain stuck in our own indecision.

A classic example is when someone wants more than anything to find the perfect job, and at the same time they do not believe that the perfect job exists. You can substitute house, car, or relationship for job. Wanting something and not believing it exists are opposing ideas. The problem is that it doesn't really matter what you want; if you hold onto the idea that what you really want does not exist, then you will never find it. When you make a conscious decision to choose "I want the perfect job for me" over "The perfect job doesn't exist," you are no longer stuck. You can choose either thought, and you will immediately become unstuck. The power is always in the decision an what you decide is always your choice.

Another example of trying to hold onto two ideas is when we think there is more than one action that needs to be taken right now. Instead of prioritizing or delegating the task, we remain stuck until we decide which to do first. To get unstuck, simply focus on one thing at a time, then move to the next idea or action. It really is impossible to think of two things at the same time. Even after years of teaching and studying the mind, I still find myself stuck on occasion in thinking I can do more than one thing at a time without asking for help. I spent years buying into the idea that multitasking was a great gift that allowed me to do more in less time than people who couldn't multitask, until I realized that multitasking was a way for me to do more of the same and remain stuck in an old paradigm that no longer served me. I am more aware now when I do this, and now when I feel stuck I simply ask myself if I am trying to do too many things at once. If the answer is yes, then I ask myself what I can delegate. What can I prioritize? And what, if anything, can I simply not do? Focus on the one thing you are willing to do, and do it.

It Happens by Law

Remember the creative process described in the chapter on imagination? First there is the fantasy, then the fantasy is turned into a theory, and then that theory is experienced as fact. The Law of Perpetual Transmutation of Energy moves your fantasy from an idea to fact through the creative process. Bob Proctor explains The Law of Perpetual Transmutation simply. He says, "Energy moves into physical form. The images that you hold in your mind most often materialize as results in your life." The creative process involves using all your intellectual faculties. Here you will see how naturally you can involve your imagination and your will in the creative process. See the diagram below.

The Creative Process

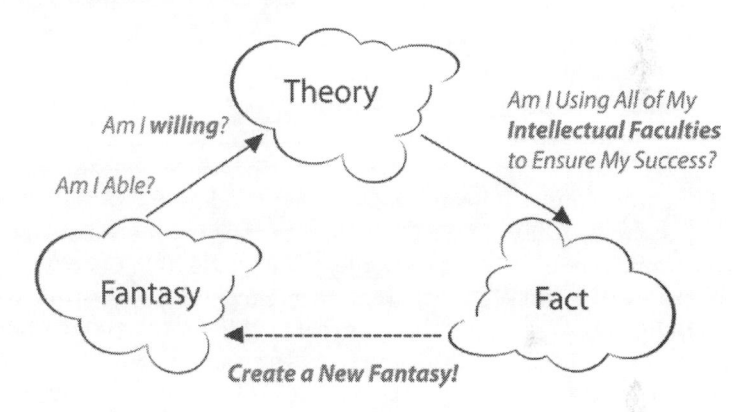

```
                    Theory
    Am I willing?              Am I Using All of My
                               Intellectual Faculties
    Am I Able?                 to Ensure My Success?


       Fantasy                      Fact
              ← - - - - - - - - -
              Create a New Fantasy!
```

Remember from the chapter on Imagination that you first start by building your fantasy. You use your imagination to build your fantasy, your desire, until you can see it as clear on the screen of your mind as you can see your reality in the physical world. Once you have your image in your mind, then ask yourself these two questions: "Am I able?" and "Am I willing?" The answer to the first question most often is, "Yes I am able." Nobody can even guess how much more you and I are able to achieve. The determining thought of the Will is "I can." You are able to do much more than you can possibly imagine. All you need to do is believe that you are able to do the thing that is here for you to do right now. Taking the little steps will always raise your awareness so you can believe you can accomplish the much bigger and seemingly impossible tasks that lie ahead. After you have aligned with the idea that you are indeed able, ask yourself the second question, "Am I willing?" This you must determine on your own. If your desire is definite and in harmony with the physical, intellectual and spiritual part of your personality, if you feel confident and calm and see clearly, you are in integrity and joy. When you see your desire clearly on the screen of your mind, you will naturally be willing to do whatever it takes to manifest your desire. However, whether you choose to take action on your idea or not is your choice. You always have a choice and both choices activate the natural Law of Attraction to bring to you whatever it is you need to fulfill your decision.

How to Effectively Use Your Will

Wallace Wattles wrote in *The Science of Getting Rich*, "Use your willpower to keep your mind off the subject of poverty, and to keep it fixed with faith and purpose on the vision of what you want." Read it again: "Use your willpower to keep your mind off the subject of poverty, and to keep it fixed with faith and purpose on the vision of what you want." Thomas Troward wrote, "The whole train of causation is started by some emotion which gives rise to a desire." Your desire is the thing you want to be, do, or have. Do you know what you want? Your vision is how it looks in your mind's eye or in your imagination. Do you have a vision of what your desire looks like? Many people have not activated their will because they haven't a clue what they really want.

The second unwritten part of the formula is to decide whether or not you are willing to have it, to do it, or to be it. The question is not, "Are you willing to do whatever you need to do, in order to get there?" The question is, "Are you willing to do the thing you wanted to do? Are you willing to be the person you desire to be? And are you willing to have the thing you desire to have? Are you willing to receive the desire?" Truthfully, most people think they are willing, yet if you ask them if they are willing to receive their desire right now, they'd say, "No! I'm not ready yet!"

Faith plays a huge part in activating your will appropriately. Without faith, you will continue to do the same things you have always done and wish for different results. With faith you know that things can and will change for you. You are willing to do things differently than you have done them in the past, and you are sure that your actions will result in the desired outcome. The more your heart is involved in your desire, the more you get swept away in the undercurrent of life itself and all your actions lead you to a place that is more than you ever imagined when you were first awakened to the desire.

Fueling Your Will

The most important part of Wattles' statement about the will is to "...keep it fixed with faith and purpose on the vision." Without a reason to want what you desire, you can easily get caught in a trap of aimlessness. You may desire many things and you may get them, however you will not be completely satisfied by your pursuits. You may know someone who seems to have it all, and yet they are depressed and unable to connect with others. This person has not used their will appropriately. Your reason does not have to be large and grandiose in order to give power and direction to your will; it can be a reason as simple as, "I want to experience myself as someone who has a loving relationship with a significant other."

Your purpose is the fuel that keeps you going. Purpose is the meaning you assign to your desire. It is the reason why you want what you want. You get to decide what meaning you add to your desire. Use your mind creatively to find meaning that moves you forward with ease and grace and allows you to let go of struggle and pain. The idea that success is hard is a misconception. Success is not hard; it can be very easy — and the more you know about yourself and how your mind works, the easier it gets. Use your will to allow your imagination to construct the mold that will become your life and have a purpose for creating that mold.

Activate Your Higher Self

When your higher self is activated, you tap into the "zone," where you are aware of your oneness with the Infinite Intelligence, with unlimited supply and nourishment in the world, and nothing can stop you. When your higher self is activated, you are one with life itself. You are energized and you step into the hypnotic rhythm of the success you seek. Anything else is simply force — and remember, force always negates. Force may move you through a wall temporarily, but at a price. The price of force is an equal and opposite force in your direction.

The reason force never works for creating lasting change is simply because you are the same person on the other side of the wall and nothing in you has changed. There is no higher purpose for such actions, and forcing them into reality only brings stress on your body and, in the end, confusion and spiritual disillusionment.

Your will is your greatest asset. It is there waiting for you to use it to transmute the energy of fear into faith so Infinite Intelligence can be accessed at will. There is no greater purpose for your will than to activate the highest vision of yourself in this very moment. Practice using your will daily. Practice transforming the energy of fear into possibility and faith, and you will find out how easy it is to let go of any habit that keeps you bound to a lower vibration, a lower plane of existence. You get to choose in this moment fear or faith. When you bring the purpose of your will to the moment you are living in right now, you choose life!

How to Know if You Are Using Your Will Appropriately

When you choose life and choose to live in alignment with your higher self, your actions take new form. Every action becomes an act of serenity and peace, you respond to the world instead of react to it, and every act you take is backed by purpose and meaning.

If you are still struggling with yourself and feel frustrated that you have not yet manifested your heart's desires, chances are you are using force, either mental or physical, to try to move yourself forward. Serenity and peace of mind are the result of using your will intelligently. If you are able to focus your attention on the activity you are doing right now and you know why you are doing it, and you trust that this moment is a perfect expression of your higher self, you are using your will constructively. If you have peace with where you are, on your way to where you are going, you are on the right track. Focus on the moment. Show up in this place and time with peace in your heart and no judgment of yourself and others. When you do this, you will benefit from your will's careful attention to your needs.

Strengthening Your Will

You can practice strengthening your will daily. There are many ways to strengthen your will, which can help you move into the right mindset to easily manifest your desires into the world and create the freedom to be yourself. You can practice using your will to guide your imagination when you are unable to act. For example, if you want to visit someone, and you are not able because you are sick or busy, sit down, relax, and mentally do it. Imagine that you are at the house of this person and visiting with him. Use your imagination to talk to him, and as you make your mental visit, relax. Though you physically may not be able to make the trip, you can do it mentally. It is imperative when you are strengthening your will that you respond to every situation with the belief that you can do everything that you want to do. Telling yourself "I can't do it" will diminish your will. The truth of your will is "I can."

The truth is you can be anything, do anything, and have anything that you want, as long as it does not diminish the life of others. From now on, any time you want to do something and have physical reasons why it seems impossible, practice seeing yourself mentally doing it. If you want to go to a party in New York, but you are obligated to attend a meeting in Seattle at the same time, take a five-minute mental party break and see yourself attending the party in New York and the meeting in Seattle. Imagine they are both successful and think, "I can do both." Then consciously choose which one you will attend and immediately make the arrangements to get there.

Your ability to strengthen your will and manifest your desires is determined by your ability to transmute energy from fear and doubt to faith and confidence by activating your desire. Use your will to think about why you want what you want. Create more reasons to motivate yourself toward success. This is growth through focused attention and purposeful use of your will. This process turns your desire into definiteness of purpose, which is an essential principle in Napoleon Hill's Think and Grow Rich. When you focus your thoughts and feelings, you enable acceleration of your growth and awareness, which allows you to manifest in an easy and effortless way.

There is no need to push or rush; you need to become aware of your definite desire and know that it comes from your higher self. Give form to it in your mind; nourish it with serenity and clarity and back up your desire with your willingness to receive. Act as if it is impossible to fail.

Be willing, focused, and calmly say, "I can." Then follow that thought immediately with action and complete the task.

Using Your Will with the Other Faculties

Your will is the facilitator that converts the habits of each of your faculties based on fear to habits based on faith and confidence. When you use your imagination to dream big, fear of acting on that big idea can creep in as a result of the paradigms held in your subconscious mind. You can use your will, then, to transform the energy of fear into the energy of faith that all things are possible.

Use your memory in the way that Nita presented it — to remember that as a child you were filled with wonder and awe about yourself and the world. You were excited about learning. You thought you could do anything. You thought you were perfect just as you were. Your will assists you when you need to transform any fears of not being enough, to faith in the memory that you were born to succeed, and born to live a life of purpose and meaning.

Your will transforms the energy of being stuck in old habits to inspired and intuitive thoughts that reveal the opportunity for you to move forward with ease and joy.

The best use of the will is to direct your attention within the constraints of the other faculties. Focus your memory on who you are and remember your greater connection to Infinite Intelligence, and be willing to maintain that state of awareness. Focus your reasoning to reveal why you want what you want and be willing to be motivated by whatever "why" you have without judgment. Focus your imagination on the perfect completed end-result with joy and enthusiasm, and again be willing to suspend judgment of the journey toward that end. Focus your perception to see every "failure" as the opportunity that it is and be willing to persist. Focus your intuition by asking the right questions; questions that lead you toward that imagined end and be willing to take action on the ideas and impulses as they come to you. When your faculties work together in this way, you have created a Mastermind. When you can bring your intellectual faculties into appropriate use in this very moment and be aware of the guid-

Your Will

ance from Infinite Intelligence in action right now, you have achieved mastery of your mind.

I always find it interesting, as I work with people at the top of their field, that they have used their will effectively to make it to the top, but they find that pushing through to the next level no longer works for them. I am passionate about helping people use their will appropriately so they come to understand that there is a much easier way to get to the top and it does not require force, it requires faith. As Victoria said, "The spoken manifestation of your will is simply, 'I can!'" You can make it easier. You can reach beyond your current level of achievement. You can expand your comfort zone and transform fear into faith!

Dawn R. Nocera, USA and SEVEN

Chapter 8

The Mastermind

Your key to multiplying power.

By Nita Matthews-Morgan and SEVEN

> "Participating in a mastermind group has been critical to me. I can't imagine achieving all I have without one, and it certainly made my goals happen much faster."
>
> ~ Jack Canfield, Chicken Soup for the Soul

In October 2010, we met each other at a Bob Proctor LifeSuccess Consulting training event held in Delray Beach, Florida. At the time, none of us knew each other or the paths that led us to this training and eventually to one another.

For four days we heard Bob Proctor teach about the unlimited power of the mind to create success. This message resonated deeply within each of us. We were excited to be in this amazing energy of like-minded people coming from all over the world to hear what Bob Proctor had to share. We all had come to this training for personal empowerment, as well as to become licensed LifeSuccess Consultants. Our days were filled with the excitement of learning and networking, and the evenings continued with passionate discussions and thinking about how we would apply this material to our own lives.

Nita shares how she was the catalyst that brought the members of SEVEN together.

"I got up very early the morning of the last day of training. I was having trouble sleeping because I knew that one of the last activities of that day was to select Mastermind groups. Not having had the chance to connect with many of the attendees because of the busy schedule, I was anxious about this task.

I started my customary early morning meditation and decided to give up my worry about who would be in my group. In this meditation, I visualized being led to other like-minded individuals who would help me hone my skills as a LifeSuccess Consultant. I asked to be led to true Mastermind partners, the persons who would be for my best and highest good; people who would support and encourage me and who would reflect the best and grandest vision of myself back to me when I couldn't see that view clearly.

Training was over, and it was time to move into action and pick people for a Mastermind. Trusting the answers revealed in meditation, I approached some of the individuals that I was guided to, and asked them to join me in a group.

Thus, the group SEVEN was born. Three of us came from the USA: myself, a college professor from Georgia; Dawn R. Nocera, a Peak Performance Coach from Ohio; and Selwa Hamati, an author, inspirational speaker and coach from California; Gwen Boudreau, a writer and visionary from Canada; Alejandro Torres-Marco, a Coach and Business owner from Mexico and Victoria Lazarova, a Personal and Corporate Executive Success Coach who lives in Bulgaria. Two continents, four countries, and three different native languages were bridged with the birth of our group.

Little did I know what I had started with my invitation. Little did I dream that out of this group would come the book that you are now reading.

You may have noticed that only six people were mentioned above yet the group is called SEVEN. The seventh mind is created from the combined minds of the others.

Masterminding is one of the most effective tools you can use to create your dreams and accelerate your success. The basic idea behind a Mastermind group, sometimes called a "dream team," is that you can achieve more in less time when you work together with other like-minded, positive people who meet regularly to discuss ideas and share information and resources.

In the chapter on Will, you read that you create your own "Mastermind" by developing your intellectual faculties for success. Developing your faculties to this extent is easier when you meet with like-minded people and follow the Mastermind principles and guidelines. According to Napoleon Hill, "No individual may have great power without availing himself of the Mastermind." Hill defined the Mastermind as the "Coordination of knowledge and effort, in a spirit of harmony, between two or more people, for the attainment of a definite purpose." This is a precise description of what happened to us. We came together as six individuals who chose to set aside ego in search of a higher purpose, and for the empowerment of each other on our individual paths of awareness and success. We also wanted to help others on this collective path to reconnect with Infinite Intelligence, experience love, and create abundance. What resulted was the creation of this book. Pretty cool, huh?

Forming a Mastermind

We encourage you to find other like-minded people to be a part of the Mastermind group so that you feel the embrace of common ideas, get support from others who believe in you, and help you envision your possibilities. Your group can help you achieve your grandest dreams, even those that still lie dormant.

When you are planning your Mastermind, it is important to choose people who are like-minded, purposeful about what they create, and willing to participate in their own growth and the growth of others in a harmonious, positive way. Not every person has to be at the same level of achievement. It is helpful to have individuals in the group who have already achieved what you would like to achieve in certain areas of your life. In turn, you can contribute to their growth in other areas.

You do not need to be friends with someone to enter into a Mastermind group. You will build your deep connection with group members as you use the Mastermind principles and connect openly. You will form a different, deeper and stronger connection than a usual friendship. Remember, the six of us did not know each other at all until the LifeSuccess event. Even then, we had only been together for less than a week before we formed our group!

Your Evolution as a Mastermind Partner

To be in a Mastermind group is to have a place where you feel appreciated, motivated, trusted, and forgiven. We all have goals, dreams and desires. We all want to be surrounded by people who are in harmony with us, who love and support us and encouraging us to grow.

Using a Mastermind and the Mastermind Principles is the way

for you to practice being a natural winner. You can build your intellectual faculties in a safe environment until they become so deeply rooted in you that you start applying them all the time in real life, even when others are not as encouraging as your "dream team" partners. You learn to become so positive and encouraging that you can transform situations around you.

Once you start seeing the rewards and the beauty of the Mastermind process, you will discover that you want to apply these principles in all areas of your life: your family, career, social life, and so on. You will learn how to see the positive in every situation and how to support and encourage others. Because of this lesson, people will be attracted to you and, sooner rather than later, you will be surrounded by caring, loving and kind people.

Victoria Lazarova shares, "My first and most successful Mastermind group experience was with people from all over the world that I had just met. I was worried about language, cultural, and individual differences. As we gradually revealed our dreams and goals with each other, we discovered that we ultimately make a powerful puzzle of knowledge and experience that is priceless and amazingly beautiful."

It quickly became apparent that each of us had a certain intellectual faculty that we were stronger in and used as our personal success tool to quickly move to higher levels of success. When we shared our personal strategy with one other, we grew individually and collectively. For instance, Gwen was excited to share her success and understanding of the imagination faculty and how it catapulted her into the field of television; Alejandro was firmly planted in using his reasoning faculty and helped us understand more easily how he uses it in his daily life to build his consulting business and his manufacturing business.

The reason most people need a team to make things happen is because they may be richer in one intellectual faculty than in others. We were able to use our intellectual strengths to easily help others in the team move forward. When we were stuck in one area and needed help, one of the others would offer a new perspective or intuitive thought. We need each other to add new awareness through other intellectual faculties until we learn to master each faculty in our own mind. In retrospect, we could see that most of the ideas we generated in the environment of our Mastermind were not just for the evolution of each project and the group itself, but also to help an individual member of the group grow. In times of individual struggle we are guided by the wisdom of the collective mind.

We use several processes to connect and support each other, and to maintain access to our higher selves. We begin our calls with a reading of the Mastermind principles, which are listed at the end of this chapter. Often we also use a short group meditation. During this guided meditation we visualize ourselves united, even though we live thousands of miles apart. As we communicate with one another on our weekly phone calls we always seek to honor each other, recognize the unlimited potential in one another, and lift each other up to the greater image we hold for each other and the group, especially when we ourselves cannot clearly access that image.

Because of the power we have experienced through masterminding, we believe that there is an answer for every problem and for every challenge. The beauty of this process is that the members of the group open themselves up in a spirit of relaxation and trust in the others, and through this trust and openness, ideas and flashes of inspiration to solve each challenge come with ease. We have all experienced times when it was difficult to see the answers to our problems and challenges. Our conditioning blinded us to creative solutions. You can release your resistance to new possibilities in the presence of others in a Mastermind group.

Why Masterminding Works

Masterminding is a process of accessing Infinite Intelligence through the combined minds of others. When you read through the Mastermind principles you will see that each member of a Mastermind group is enriched and empowered, and a "Master Mind" is created from the combined intelligence of all the group members. As you connect to inspiration, what you create as a result of a Mastermind is much greater than what you can do alone.

The most important thing is that you enter into the Mastermind group to give. Masterminding recognizes and accepts that you personally do not have all the answers for yourself, but you may have answers that others need. Participating in a Mastermind is submitting to a process where Infinite Intelligence is allowed to flow through so that every person is called to act as his or her higher self.

Can you imagine the power of six minds combined? Six minds who earnestly yearned to be connected to Infinite Intelligence and to be a channel of the most inspired thoughts possible?

When you allow access to the power of your higher self then you may realize that struggle becomes something of the past. You can break the habit of having to push your way through or having to "try hard." Accessing Infinite Intelligence with your thoughts and images frees your creative inspiration, which can lead to blissful action. You no longer have to act stubbornly to do what you want or need to do. Instead, you can gently use your will to focus and concentrate on a better thought or a happier feeling, knowing this feeling will lead to a more inspired action.

As the six of us willingly have the intention of being connected to our higher selves and Infinite Intelligence, and submit ourselves to creative inspiration, we experience the exhilaration of having the Mastermind — the seventh mind in our group — pour through us in a new way. There are times when one of us has a brilliant idea, an idea that resonates with the other members of our group. Each of us plays an individual and important role in this process because there is always one of us who can see the better path, the intelligent way forward so we can take the easy and effortless path to freedom and joy.

All of us have been in, and at times facilitated, other Mastermind groups, yet we have never experienced the powerful creations that resulted from this group that we call SEVEN. We have never before Masterminded with a group of individuals who worked on a common goal, such as creating a webinar, program, and book. Having a common goal helped us reorganize our individual agendas. In every group there is the possibility of tension arising from attachment to egos and for the need to be in control. Yes, there were times when we functioned from our old paradigms and belief systems, when we were stuck in our egos and had difficulty seeing a different point of view, but we trusted the process and knew that we were moving toward a common goal which reflected a higher purpose.

Being in this group means facing fears and having the courage and encouragement to step into our grander selves while going through individual and collective paradigm shifts. In times of individual struggle we are guided by the wisdom of the collective mind.

With the urging of each other to let go of our need to be in control and to enjoy the process, we were able to accomplish things previously considered impossible: to write, present, and stretch beyond our self-imposed limits.

You can change one small habit and change your life. We set aside an hour and a half each week for this group. In that time, we brainstorm to produce ideas and to solve problems, and we inspire and conspire for each other's success. During one of our calls we were discussing what these calls do for us personally and Gwen said, "I am so inspired and motivated after our calls that sometimes I can't sleep that night! If I am in a dark place, you always lift me up so that I may see my higher self. I have accomplished more than I ever thought possible because of our Mastermind group."

We all agree that as a Mastermind group we are always greater than our individual parts, and that the synergy of our collective growth is amazing. Victoria said, "The principle of the Mastermind has given me one of the biggest lessons in my life: to be open and trust people and to become fully aware that I can advance in life only if I take others with me on my journey of success."

Masterminding is a success practice that always works. Applying the Mastermind principles and guidelines with faith and dedication will give you rewards beyond measure.

MASTERMIND PRINCIPLES

Begin every Mastermind Meeting by reading these Mastermind Principles:

I RELEASE
I release myself to the Mastermind because I am strong when I have others to help me.

I BELIEVE
I believe the combined intelligence of the Mastermind creates a wisdom far beyond my own.

I UNDERSTAND
I understand that I will more easily create positive results in my life when I am open to looking at problems, my opportunities and myself from another's point of view.

I DECIDE
I decide to release my desire totally in trust to the Mastermind (and I am open to accepting new possibilities).

I FORGIVE
I forgive myself for mistakes I have made. I also forgive others who have hurt me in the past so I can move into the future with a clean slate.

I ASK
I ask the Mastermind to hear what I really want; my goals, my dreams and my desires, and I hear my Mastermind partners supporting me in my fulfillment.

I ACCEPT
I know, relax and accept, believing that the working power of the Mastermind will respond to my every need. I am grateful knowing this is so.

DEDICATION AND COVENANT
"I now have a covenant in which it is agreed that the Mastermind shall supply me with an abundance of all things necessary to live a success-filled and happy life. I dedicate myself to be of maximum service to God and my fellow human beings, to live in a manner that will set the highest example for others to follow and to remain an open channel of God's will. I go forth with a spirit of enthusiasm, excitement and expectancy."

MASTERMIND GUIDELINES

1. The average group works best with two to eight members, but no more than 12 — time is the constraint. Most people find that six is ideal.

2. Meet regularly, weekly if possible, for an hour to an hour and a half. Group members need to see this meeting as a sacred commitment. They agree to be encouraging and positive and to share information, ideas, contacts and feedback for the good of each individual and the good of the group.

3. Meet in a nice, preferably inspirational place if possible. Make sure it is a well-lit restaurant, office, home, library or church etc. Have a preplanned agenda.

4. If you are in different cities, the meeting can be conducted on a conference call. Make certain you engage an excellent conference call company (setting up a series of 3-way calls does not work well.) You might save a few pennies but miss a million-dollar opportunity through distractions.

5. Start the meetings by reading the Mastermind principles. This is possibly one of the most important points of a call. Every member of the group should read aloud all seven principles and the dedication and covenant.

6. The others should support each member visually, verbally and emotionally. For example: someone wants a new home. Other members might say, "I see you driving up to your glorious new home. I see you sunning yourself at poolside with your loved ones, friends and me." The principle is that we can believe for others what they cannot fully believe for themselves. These are not idle words. You must create and project to the Mastermind a clear vision that the words represent

7. Your Mastermind call should run like a Swiss watch. Be sure the call is timely. If you have committed to a 60-minute call,

keep it within that timeframe. Mastermind members are generally extremely busy, and time is important. Use it wisely.

8. It's important that everyone gets the same amount of time if you want your group to last. Each group should elect a time-keeper to keep everything flowing freely. This position can rotate from one member to another. The time-keeper should be prepared to time each person's participation in the call to ensure it is kept on track. Have a watch (with a second hand) or stop watch available. This point is extremely important (do not treat it lightly).

9. Roll call: the group leader would take a roll call and would assign each person a number (i.e., if there are six people on the call, each person would have a number from 1-6). This numbering system can be used to designate who speaks when and should be rotated with each call to ensure the #1 person doesn't always speak first.

10. Good news: starting with whichever number is designated for that particular meeting, each person would be allowed two minutes to speak about something very positive. They will share their "win for the week." This will help to get the meeting started in a positive direction.

11. Wants and needs: again, starting with whichever number has been designated to begin first, each person would have 10 minutes (the group would decide on the length of time) in which to state their wants and needs and receive their responses. It might sound like, "This is John. This is what I want and this is what I need." Or, "This is John. This is a challenge I'm facing and I would appreciate the help of my Mastermind group." It's important that everyone understands that the designated amount of time allotted is both to state their want/need and to receive the group's response. Therefore, if four minutes has been designated to each person and someone is not prepared to share and it takes them three and 1/2 minutes to state what they need, it allows the group only a 1/2-minute to respond. Each Mastermind member needs to be prepared

with their part to ensure maximum benefit. At the end of the four minutes, it would be the team leader's responsibility to say, "Time is up." The discussion would then come to a halt. The second person would be asked to begin.

12. Depending on the "chosen" length of your meeting or call, you may decide to leave room for a "free-for-all" at the end, at which time anyone and everyone would have a chance to speak. End by sharing appreciations and acknowledgements.

Nita Matthews-Morgan and SEVEN

Chapter 9

Your Awareness

Accessing the wisdom of your Higher Self.

By *Nita Matthews-Morgan* and *SEVEN*

"The primary cause of unhappiness is never the situation but your thoughts about it. Be aware of the thoughts you are thinking. Separate them from the situation, which is always neutral. It is as it is."
~ Eckhart Tolle

Using your intellectual faculties will help you increase your awareness — your awareness of the power of your thought, your awareness of your old conditioning and how limiting it can be, and ultimately your awareness of your unlimited power as a human being. We want you to become more aware of your thoughts so that you can see how they create your reality. Once you gain that awareness, you realize that some of your thoughts help you grow and some keep you stuck in a life you don't like. You will also learn that you are not alone on this journey to full expression.

We want to help you increase your awareness of your unlimited potential as a creative being. We believe that you were born perfect. Despite the environment you might have been born in, you can improve every aspect of your life. Making the decision to really learn and internalize these ideas will profoundly change your life. You will be open to new possibilities, eager about life and enthusiastic to create the desires that burn inside of you.

Most people believe that the situations in which they were born is where they should stay. They are trapped by family, friends, and paradigms, and often see no chance of improving their conditions. They have no idea how their thinking affects their results and even more, no clue about having intellectual faculties. They live unaware, within the mental prison created by their conditioning. Alejandro described himself before he became aware of his intellectual faculties:

I knew that I had a memory, and that I'd better use it, otherwise I would be in trouble at school and at home for not remembering my assignments and chores. I knew that I had an imagination, but people told me it was best not to use it so I could always keep my feet on the ground. I also knew I had a will. At the time, what others said about the will was very confusing. On one hand, they told me we all had free will. But I always got punished when I used it because they said I "misused" it. Others told me that reason should only be used to determine the difference between right or wrong. Of course, many times I made the wrong decision.

Perception and intuition were not even part of my vocabulary. The first time I remember hearing about intuition was listening to adults talk about mediums and Gypsies. In my mind, intuition was definitely a feminine thing, so I couldn't have cared less about it. In other words, I was not aware of the huge difference my intellectual faculties could have in my growth, and therefore in my life. Even though I started using some of them at a young age, I was not really aware that they were intellectual faculties and could be developed like a muscle in my body.

In the past, you may have acted on your thoughts without knowing that you had a choice. You reacted because of a negative memory of the past or a negative perception of a person, event or circumstance. Perhaps, now you know that awareness of your thoughts gives you the chance to decide whether your thoughts, memories or perceptions are true.

Becoming Aware of the Voice in your Mind

> "There is nothing more important to true growth than realizing that you are not the voice of the mind - you are the one who hears it." ~ Eckhart Tolle

Your inner speech is what creates your outer reality. It is responsible for creating what you want, or more of the circumstances that you don't want. If your inner speech focuses on what has been in the past or on what is missing in your life, then you will create more of that. What you focus on expands in your life. It is inevitable, and it is also wonderful, because you are in control of your thoughts, and you can use the power of your own mind any time you want. It is yours, and nobody can take it away from you.

Before we were aware that we could choose our thoughts, we were slaves to the ideas we got from other people and past experiences. Our inner speech was shaped almost exclusively by others. We often reacted blindly to what people said and to events that "happened" to us. We had no idea that we did not have to live the way our parents did or that we could fulfill our own dreams. We believed that the thoughts in our head were the only truth, and that we had to act or respond to them. However, acting upon old negative feelings and thoughts will not bring the success you want. You will create more of what you already have in your life if you do not change the thoughts and images that do not serve you.

You cannot change your thoughts unless you are aware of them. Becoming aware of your thoughts is the first important step in your journey to freedom. You can do this by becoming aware that you have a voice in your head that controls how you think, feel, and act. The voice in your head is usually your old conditioning, but when you distance yourself from that voice, you become more aware of what you are thinking, which frees you to apply your intellecual faculties. From this perspective, you have the freedom to step back from your thoughts and realize that they do not control you. Becoming aware of your thoughts means you now have an opportunity to choose what you think and believe. You realize that negative thoughts, memories, or images cloud your perception of events and circumstances so that you see problems instead of opportunities. You are aware when you no longer blindly trust information from your senses as your only reality, because you know there is more in the picture that you may not see. You can shift your focus to what you really want for your life, even if it is a mental image that hasn't shown up yet.

You have taken a massive step when you become aware that you have thoughts, but they are not you. You are the master of your thoughts, not their victim. Moreover, the bigger part of you exists beyond your daily thoughts.

It is easy to know what you are thinking because you have a voice in your head that is always talking. It's like a radio station that you cannot turn off because the "off" button is broken. It is saying things to you right now as you read this sentence. It might be saying things like, "What are you talking about? I am not some crazy person who hears voices!" And you have probably noticed that you have a mental dialogue going on inside of your head all the time. We all do. You hear this voice when you are tired and trying to go to sleep. It says things like, "I really need to get some sleep because I have that important presentation tomorrow. I still haven't prepared for it. Oh no, I forgot that I have to pick up my son from the airport tomorrow! That means I won't have time to get ready tomorrow so maybe I should get up now and prepare. Boy, I really need to sleep! Why am I thinking about this stuff when I'm so tired? Now I really can't sleep. I'm going to be so tired tomorrow that I'll probably do a terrible job. Things will be really bad if I don't make that sale. I've got to get some sleep."

The voice in your head will even carry on both sides of a conversation. You can hear it talking when you have a decision to make, and you drive yourself crazy presenting pros and cons for each possible scenario. This voice will go on and on, taking both sides of the conversation. This inner voice really doesn't care which side it takes; it just wants to keep on talking.

The voice in your head is trying to help you solve your life problems. The trouble is that you have given it an impossible task. Your voice will say things that match your current beliefs, which might not help you solve a problem or see an opportunity. You will be trying to solve your problems using your old conditioning.

Sometimes you use your intellectual faculties without awareness. For example, you use your memory, intuition, reason, perception, imagination, and will as you try to make a decision. As you talk to yourself inside your head, your mind replays memories of past decisions, and struggles to know the truth--whether you are reasoning from intuition or paradigms. Your mind considers and ranks different alternatives and actions, creates pictures of what could happen in the future, and tries mightily to perceive the best path you can take. You will yourself to keep this up even though it is very busy inside your mind. After a lot of mental chatter, you end up feeling exhausted.

Your journey to freedom means letting go of some of this chatter so you can access your subconscious mind, as well as your conscious mind. Perhaps you remember from the Memory chapter how children's brains evolve from lower to higher brain wave frequencies, from theta (subconscious) to beta (conscious) brain waves. Your developmental journey as a child was from the subconscious to the conscious mind. Now, on your road to freedom, you want to go backwards, to reclaim your access to your subconscious mind. You want to be able, at times, to let go of the constraints of the conscious mind and play in the fields of your subconscious. Just imagine connecting with the creative possibilities that you so easily accessed as a child!

As adults, we think that focusing intently on our problems is the only way to get results. However, when we are stuck in beta brain wave frequencies, we are usually obsessing about problems instead of becoming aware of solutions. Very little new information can get in because of our narrow focus. You will know when you're in beta when you are constantly analyzing and perhaps experiencing "paralysis by analysis."

You cannot effectively solve your problems using your mind until you become aware of your thoughts. You will know from the conversation in your head whether you are using your intellectual faculties to grow or whether you are using your old ways of thinking to stay stuck in your situation. You will know by how you feel. As you have read in the previous chapters, feelings give you a clue to the thoughts you are thinking, and, therefore, the results you create. If your feelings are of lack and scarcity, then that is your old conditioning. If you feel small and inadequate, then you can be sure that your inner voice is beating you up with past mistakes or thoughts that you most likely learned from other people. If you feel doubt and fear, then you are focusing on old, limiting thinking.

How do you think and feel when you are leaning toward growth? You think about where you are going, not where you are right now. You ignore present reality as you focus on what you are creating. You feel hopeful, expansive, and powerful. You choose belief over doubt.

Watching your thoughts helps you apply your intellectual faculties in a way that helps you grow. The more you distance yourself from your limiting thoughts, the more aware you are that you exist beyond your thinking. Meditation helps you get quiet inside and shift from the beta brain waves of over-focused, stressed attention to the relaxed, slow brain waves of theta as you open the door from your conscious mind to your subconscious mind. Once you're there, you will be able to hear the gentle voice of loving wisdom, the voice of Infinite Intelligence. When you are there, you can use your inner voice to stay focused on what you intend to create, and you will find yourself connecting to the power of this intelligence, and to your unlimited potential. As Dr. Dispenza explains in *Breaking the Habit of Being Yourself*:

> Your awareness shifts from narrow-minded, overfocused, obsessive, compartmentalized, survival thinking to thoughts that are more open, relaxed, holistic, present, orderly, creative, and simple. This is the natural state of being we are supposed to live by.

Your Seven Levels of Awareness

You will go through a continuum of awareness on your way to freedom. Once you reach one level it does not mean you won't fall back at times to a lower, less aware level. It is not a college diploma that, once you achieve it, you can hang on the wall and be done with it. But as you continue to grow in your ability to use your intellectual faculties, you will become a master of yourself and of your thoughts. You can learn to master your creative power just like you learned how to ride a bike or drive a car. You just have to practice.

The lower extreme of this continuum reflects the times when you reacted blindly without thought. You know it because you do not feel free at this level. You replay memories from your past that do not serve you, and you take in information from your environment through your five senses. When you are just seeing, hearing, and reacting, you are reacting by default. You feel thrown about because everyone has an opinion, and you don't know which opinion to believe. When situations are not going well you do not thrive because your thoughts match these circumstances.

The higher end of the continuum represents freedom to create what you want in your life. You are free from your negative thoughts and memories. You are free from your circumstances. You are free to create memories of success and thoughts that lead you to create your dreams. When you gain control of your thinking you can thrive in the best of times and in the worst of times. You are aware that you can

create things that are different from outside reality.
Our thoughts and feelings show where we are on this continuum of awareness. Knowing where you are on this scale may help you determine how close you are to being free. The more you become aware of your thoughts and the more you can direct your thoughts, the higher up the scale of awareness you climb.

The first level of awareness is *animalistic*. Here we react, without thinking, out of our fight or flight response, much like animals do. We have knee-jerk reactions to life. For example, we react instinctively to protect ourselves when feeling threatened by what someone says. If they insult us, we either immediately insult them back or retreat and fume without dealing assertively with the situation. We do not have the freedom to choose what we want when we respond without thinking. Just like animals, we don't have the perspective that we can be aware of, and direct our thoughts so we can choose how to act. At this level, we do not have power over our lives; we are like robots — people push our buttons and we oblige!

The second level is *mass awareness*. At this level we do something because everyone else is doing it. When we act out of mass awareness, we rarely think for ourselves. We usually are not aware of our thoughts and we don't analyze the reasons for our behavior. Much of what we call thinking is just mental activity where we replay what we hear others say, what we see on television, and what we read in the paper. We know we are at this level when we think like everyone else around us. We may have accepted religious or political beliefs from our family and environment without questioning them. We may not know that we can be different. We also are not aware that we can choose different information than what we receive from our senses to make our decisions. For example, a person may watch the news about the economy tanking and decide to stay in a job that they hate even though they have a great business idea, or they work as an accountant because their father and grandfather were accountants. They stay in their career even though it is not their dream or passion.

You move into the third level of awareness, *aspiration*, as you begin to be aware of yourself as a unique person and aspire to become your fullest self. You want the freedom that comes from detaching from your thoughts and from the expectations and plans of others. You become more aware of the limiting paradigms you have accepted from your culture and environment. You begin to re-evaluate these beliefs as you create a new set of beliefs aimed toward growth — the growth that you are entitled to as a birthright. Even as you move toward independence of thought, there are still times when you fall back into reacting blindly or not thinking for yourself.

Aspiring to be free from limiting beliefs will move you into the fourth level of awareness, the *individual* level. This is where you now feel free to express your own individuality. You leave your comfort zone as you develop your own unique path. As you become aware that there is no one like you, you realize the value you bring when you really function from your own uniqueness. You start creating rather than competing with others. You are aware of what the majority is doing, yet you choose to map out your own path in spite of criticism from others. At this level you become more aware of your thoughts and their power over your emotions, behavior and results.

You are at the *focus* level, level five, as you decide to follow your unique path and as you develop your intellectual faculties. You discipline yourself to stay the course and keep going, even when the road seems hard. To gain strength, you surround yourself with like-minded people who support your unique way of thinking. Their willingness to follow their own path encourages you to do the same. The image of what you want, your "why," pulls you forward during times when you are not sure if you are on the right path. For example, I retired from my college teaching career to start a new business as a performance coach. Even though the early goings were a struggle, connecting with my purpose as I was building my business helped me continue my journey. I realized that I wanted the thrill of growth and expansion that comes from leaving my comfort zone, and I wanted to help others experience the excitement of expanding their own awareness.

A focused individual will create new behaviors and paradigms that support growth and positive circumstances. At this level of awareness, you will find it easier to give yourself a command and follow it. You choose to think for yourself instead of thinking like others. As you become even more aware of old thoughts and behaviors that pull you away from your goals, you choose to act according to new thoughts of growth and freedom. You are aware that you can let your old paradigms control your life or you can step into the freedom of thinking for yourself.

You move into the sixth level of awareness, *experience*, the more you learn to enjoy your journey. You are willing to learn lessons along the way. Knowing that mistakes are only lessons, you decide to experience and learn from every part of your journey on your way to success. You do more of what works in your life and less of what doesn't work, and you learn to honor who you are at every step of the way.

There is an old saying, "When fear knocks on the door, faith opens it, and suddenly there is nobody there." Even when old, limiting paradigms knock on your door, you practice faith, deciding to act from positive paradigms that lead to freedom. Limiting paradigms cannot last long when you use discipline and focus. The process of confronting your paradigms and continuing growth leads you to the seventh level of awareness: mastery.

At the *mastery* level, you find it easier to live in integrity with your desires and your higher self. You realize that this journey toward awareness is a daily practice. You know that you do not "arrive"; you are growing and learning all the time. At this level, your buttons are no longer being pushed and you are living on purpose. You are aware that you are greater than your thoughts. You are aware of the power of your thoughts, and you know when your thoughts are in tune with Infinite Intelligence and thoughts of abundance, or with old, limiting conditioning. You know how to distance yourself from thoughts created by old conditioning. Even though you still feel negative emotions you choose to redirect your thoughts so you can feel better. You are free to change them to help you create what you want.

These levels represent a continuum of freedom. There will be times when you do not feel free, when fear and anxiety keep you in your comfort zone. You may feel that you have slipped back into a more basic level of reacting rather than acting on life. Do not worry, because you always have the choice of becoming more aware of what you are thinking, and choosing another thought if you don't like the tense knot in your stomach and the results you are getting. You can always seek freedom. Do not look to other people or outward circumstances to give you freedom, for that is slavery. Instead, seek freedom inside — in your mind. It is slavery to allow others to control you and your life.

The pull of our old paradigms, and our old way of thinking, is strong. Limiting paradigms will try to trap you with the logic of staying where you are. They will especially give you grief when you decide to step into new territory and act on what you really want. Recognize that beliefs are just thoughts that you have practiced a lot. Old beliefs will enslave you until you practice new thoughts and they become your new beliefs. Masterminding with others who are striving for freedom will speed you through these levels of awareness.

We know that the path to freedom is easier when you develop your intellectual faculties — imagination, memory, reason, perception, intuition, and will. Start perceiving the world as conspiring to help you achieve your dreams, and then you will use your reason to think only of possibilities. Memories of prior successes will flood your mind and help create new images of success. You will trust your intuitive nudges and flashes of insight coming from your feelings that point you in the direction of what you really want. You will use your will to focus on your purpose and to maintain the clearest vision of yourself experiencing the best possible outcome that you can imagine.

The more you use your intellectual faculties, the more you become aware of your divine guidance.

Awareness of Infinite Intelligence

"As a man who has devoted his whole life to the most clear-headed science, to the study of matter, I can tell you as the result of my research about atoms this much: there is no matter as such! All matter originates and exists only by virtue of a force which brings the particles of an atom to vibration and holds this most minute solar system of the atom together...We must assume behind this force the existence of a conscious and intelligent mind. This mind is the matrix of all matter."
~ Max Plank, Nobel prize-winning physicist

We ask you to consider that the ultimate expression of freedom comes from the realization that you are inhabited by a universal power. Whether this force is called God, Jesus, Allah, Buddha, Source, or any number of other names does not matter. You may be comfortable believing in one of these images or you may see yourself as part of the stream of Infinite Intelligence. You may also choose to believe that there is no universal force conspiring for your good.

Whatever your beliefs, we would like to point out that there is no downside to believing in something greater than yourself. You could spend much time arguing against the idea of the Divine or trying to prove it, or you could relax and entertain the thought that there is a universal power that guides you to ever-expanding visions of yourself.

Your path to awareness will get smoother as you realize you are not alone on this journey. You were born with Infinite Intelligence. You are not able to separate yourself from this fact even if you choose not to accept it. Infinite Intelligence was breathed along with life into you at birth. It continues to call you forward toward the fullest manifestation of yourself, and it guides and supports you through every waking moment. It is only your lack of awareness that keeps you from accessing a power greater than yourself, one that will help you fulfill your potential.

When you become aware and act upon the premise that you are a part of Infinite Intelligence, you take action in your fullness as a human being. Your ability to create is magnified hugely because you have an awareness of greater resources available to you. Imagine yourself being able to easily access the energy and ideas of solutions instead of problems. Imagine creating your life from the awareness of all possibilities. Imagine sharing that power with other people who are also creating from this awareness.

Trusting in a power greater than yourself to provide the "how," "what," and "where" of what you need to create your dreams frees you to focus mainly on your "why." In other words, you do not need to know all the details of what you want before you get started. Focusing on your purpose, your "why," helps you get started. All the other details will fall into place as you take inspired action. And inspiration comes from Infinite Intelligence through the doorway of your intuition.

When you allow access to the power of your infinite and intelligent nature, then you may realize that struggle becomes something of the past. You can break the habit of having to push your way through, using effort or "trying hard." Accessing Infinite Intelligence through your intellectual faculties frees your creative inspiration, which can lead to correct action. You no longer have to use "willpower" to do what you want or need to do. Instead, you can gently tune your focus and concentration to a better thought, a happier feeling, knowing this feeling will lead to more inspired action.

The awareness of yourself as an integral part of Infinite Intelligence will be greatly enhanced by the use of your intellectual faculties. Using your mind to focus on your heart's desires becomes your stairway to freedom and excellence. You are free to see yourself as the being that you are - a person with unlimited potential, the creator of your own reality. You are free from the bondage of limiting thoughts and beliefs, free from living and feeling small.

You develop your awareness as you develop your intellectual faculties. Awareness is empowerment. When you are aware of how you create, you are empowered. If you are not aware of the infinite power that your intellectual faculties will provide you, then you will continue to believe that your current results are the limit of what you can do or be. You will be unaware of the power of your imagination to create what you want, even if it is something far from what you see in your present reality. Remember the phrase "I'll believe it when I see it?" That phrase describes someone who is unaware of their intellectual faculties. It may describe how you functioned in the past. With awareness of the power of your thoughts you can create what you believe rather than being left with creating more of what you see. When you master your intellectual faculties you become aware of the creative power inside you. You are confident in your ability to create. Suddenly everything becomes clear and bright. Awareness is like turning on the light in a dark room and seeing a clear and bright new world in front of your eyes.

Conclusion

We have grown so much as authors and people through the process of creating this book. Let me assure you that we are not the same people as when we first started this journey. Writing this book took us way beyond our comfort zone, pushed us to grow, and helped us to become more aware of our unlimited potential to create, not only as SEVEN, but individually as well. We have become more alive.

You become more fully alive as you strive to fulfill your potential and bring your gifts to the world. You are following Howard Thurman's wise advice: "Don't ask what the world needs. Ask what makes you come alive, and go do it. Because what the world needs are people who have come alive." As you become more alive you become extraordinary. You will want to share yourself with others as you give more to the world. According to Jacques Yves Cousteau, "When one man, for whatever reason, has the opportunity to lead an extraordinary life, he has no right to keep it to himself."

Since this book is about freedom, we asked ourselves, what is the ultimate freedom? We have described in prior chapters the freedom to be able to create what you want in your life, which means giving up fear and anxiety. So we asked ourselves, "What does it feel like to step into a place with no fear?" The answer was immediate: the ultimate freedom is to experience joy!

We believe that our ultimate purpose on this Earth is to experience joy. As you experience joy you are living from your highest potential and giving the world the gift of yourself.

We experience joy through connection to Infinite Intelligence. All the things you want — more money, happy relationships, and better health — give you a chance to fill up with joy. A new car, house, or boat are great things to have; however, if you see them as the source of your joy, these things will only satisfy you for a short while. What we really yearn for is this deeper connection to something greater than ourselves and to our unlimited potential. Nothing else satisfies us because all else fades in comparison to that deeper connection.

When you feel the joy of living to your full potential, you are touching Infinite Intelligence. We feel joy when we experience our full potentiality in our physical bodies. Pay attention to those moments when you are in the middle of a luminous moment of joy. It could be when you are hugging a child or when you are in the middle of a meeting when everything clicks. This moment is enough. In this moment, you connect to yourself and to Infinite Intelligence.

Our intention is that we all find our own strength, live our highest purpose, serve with the gifts we were given, and make a difference in the world. We refuse to believe that it is not possible! It is possible! We have a vision that all of us are luminaries, and as luminaries we must provide light to others as they also seek abundance, health, companionship, and joy.

We would like to leave you with some words that Dawn shared one morning in an email to the rest of SEVEN. We hope these words will inspire you as much as they inspired us:

I am abundance. I am health. I am happiness. I am faith.
I am joy. My eyes see nothing else. My ears hear nothing else.
My lips speak nothing else. My mind thinks nothing else. My hands hold only to that truth. My nostrils are full of the sweet smell of beauty in every step I take.
I taste the sweetness of my perfection and the perfection of others as I drink from the fullness of Spirit.

~ Dawn R. Nocera

With Love and Gratitude,
Nita Matthews-Morgan and SEVEN

Author Bios

Gwen Boudreau is the co-author of *10 Powerful Women* in addition to this book. She has studied with, and is mentored by, one of today's living masters of Mind Potential, Mr. Bob Proctor, best know for his commentary in the best selling book and movie *The Secret*. A visionary leader, Gwen is dedicated to helping women develop an authentic and successful self-image so they can break through their fears and achieve their dreams.

She founded Punch Bowl Productions in 2008 where she creates and develops projects for both film and television, which incorporates her love of personal development with her passion for empowering women. She repeatedly jokes that she is pathologically optimistic and frequently finds the humor in life's most challenging moments. Gwen celebrates her life in Nova Scotia, Canada with her 3 beautiful children. In her spare time she loves to run, read, write and travel with her friends and family.

Please visit Gwen's website to learn more about her and her work: www.GwenBoudreau.com

Selwa Hamati is an Author, Inspirational Speaker and LifeSuccess Consultant.

After being personally impacted by applying the knowledge and practices acquired through the self help industry, and as a LifeSuccess Consultant, Selwa Hamati committed herself to life-long learning so she can continue to grow and expand her mind while helping her clients do the same. As part of her learning and growth strategy, as well as her ongoing passion to help others, Selwa became a Neuro-Linguistic Programming Practitioner, and Quit Smoking Specialist (NLP & Hypnotherapy practitioner, certified through the Association for Integrative Psychology). It is her intention to help as many people as possible to achieve their goals and live a full and abundant life.

Selwa Hamati is the author of "Once Upon a Recession" — Facing the new economic realities with passion, purpose, and commitment to succeed; and co-author of "10 Powerful Women"--10 Strategic Insights into Successful Business.

Please visit Selwa's website to learn more about her and her work: www.SelwaHamati.com.

Author Bios

Victoria Lazarova is a Professional Business Executive & Personal Success Coach. She works with individuals and teams, helping them to ultimately grow their business and truly enjoy every day of their new life. People develop their ability to think into results, have new perceptions of the world, and access new resources within them. She specializes in facilitating change by helping individuals and companies create a new self-image that makes winning in business and life an easy routine rather than an accident.

Victoria has studied with, and is mentored by, one of today's living masters of Mind Potential, Mr. Bob Proctor. Certified Life Success Coach with Life Success Productions; NLP Practitioner & Hypnotherapy practitioner with the American Association of Integrative Psychology, She also holds a Master's degree in Finance. In addition to this book, she is also the co-author of *10 Powerful Women*.

Victoria received the award of Business Lady of the Year for 2011 in Sofia, Bulgaria, in the category Life Coaching. She is a founder & Chairman of the Association of Happy & Powerful Women in Bulgaria.

For more information about Victoria and her work, please visit: www.VictoriaLazarova.com and www.PraxisSuccess.com.

Nita Matthews-Morgan, Ph.D. is a speaker, performance coach and co-founder of Polaris Performance Coaching. Holding a PhD in Educational Psychology with an emphasis in Creativity and Creative Problem Solving, she has taught college classes in cognition, creativity, human development and research. As Director of the Torrance Center for Creative Studies, she sponsored the International Future Problem Solving Conference, where children from across the world learned how to solve problems and become future leaders.

Presently, Nita combines her expert knowledge of the brain and creativity, along with a mixture of playful fun, to help others connect to their potential so they can be at the top of their game in life and business. Her passion is nurturing the success of others. Nita is thrilled to have founded Polaris Performance Coaching with one of her sons, Josh, a company that helps individuals and business teams set and achieve goals. They have co-authored the book *Deliver*, a guide for achieving the mindset for peak performance. In her spare time she enjoys being in nature, writing, traveling, dabbling in art and music and spending time with her family.

Please visit Nita's website to learn more about her and her work: www.PolarisPerformanceCoaching.com.

Author Bios

Dawn R Nocera, is an authentic wealth attraction mindset mentor, and transformational coach featured in the DVD, A Spiritual Approach to Unlimited Abundance, and creator of "Your 12 Seeds of Wealth: Sowing the 12 Seeds of Authentic Wealth & Happiness" coaching program. Her message, "There is an easy and effortless path to success, but few are brave enough to travel it!" has awakened many sleeping giants. Dawn has worked with entrepreneurs and industry leaders in the top 1% of their fields, including consulting for MTV's MADE, a World Champion of Public Speaking, and has been featured on PBS for her work with young women."

Dawn uses her gifts of intuition and insight into success to guide her clients through breakthrough transformations. She helps align your businesses and lifes with your most natural path to authentic wealth. Her gentle approach to success is a welcome breath of fresh air when you are ready to stop chasing butterflies and start attracting what you really want in life!"

For more information about Dawn and her work, please visit: www.DawnNocera.com

Alejandro Torres-Marco is a Professional Corporate Keynote Speaker and Corporate Personal Growth Development Consultant.

With a speciality in human potential development, Alejandro is an N.L.P. Training Practitioner and a Memory Development Trainer.

Alejandro is also a Biologist with specialties in Commercial Diving, Business Administration, Finance-Accounting, Network System Telecommunications, Solar Renewable Systems, and Human Potential Development.

His passion is teaching people how to achieve whatever they want. He can't wait to share this wonderful personal growth knowledge.

To learn more about Alejandro, visit his website: www.ActitudyCrecimientoPersonal.com

The Seventh Author is the Mastermind

"No two minds ever come together without, thereby, creating a third, invisible, intangible force which may be likened to a third mind." ~ Napoleon Hill

Although there are only six of us, we call ourselves SEVEN. It is clear to us that soon after forming our group and formulating a common purpose, we had created a true mastermind. The Seventh Author, the Mastermind, is the real hero of this book. Accessed only by joining of the six other minds in the spirit of cooperation and harmony, the Seventh Mind took over in times of doubt and worry to lead our way toward ultimate freedom--freedom from fear. Only through accessing this Seventh Mind were we able to trust that our book, *7 Keys to Freedom*, would safely reach your hands. It is to this seventh Mind that we dedicate this book.

For more information about the Group of SEVEN, please go to: www.7KeystoFreedom.com

References

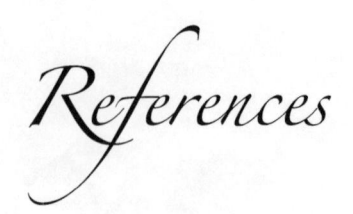

The Mind

Allen, James. *As a Man Thinketh*. Radford, VA: Wilder Publications, 2007.

Amen, Daniel. *Change Your Brain, Change Your Life*. New York, NY, Three Rivers Press, 1998.

Branden, Nathaniel. *The Six Pillars of Self-Esteem*. New York, New York: Bantam Books, 1995.

Deaton, Dennis. *The Othello Principle: The Eye Sees What the Mind Looks for*. Mesa, AZ: Quma Learning Systems, Inc, 2002.

Dyer, Wayne. *The Power of Intention*. Carlsbad, California: Hay House, Inc, 2005.

Fleet, Thurman. Quoted by Bob Proctor, *The Winner's Image Program*. LifeSuccess Productions, LLC. 1995.

Rohn, Jim. Weekend Seminar. Skills for the 21st Century.

Imagination

Begley, Sharon. *The Brain: How the Brain Rewires Itself*. Time Magazine. January 19, 2007.

Behrend, Genevieve. *Your Invisible Power*. Radford, VA: Wilder Publications. 2008.

Byrne, Rhonda. *The Secret*. New York, NY: Atria Books. 2006.

Hill, Napoleon. *Think and Grow Rich*. Rockville, Maryland: ARC Manor, 2007.

Maltz, Maxwell. *Psycho-Cybernetics*. New York, NY: Pocket Books, 1960.

Proctor, Bob. *The Winner's Image Program*. LifeSuccess Productions, LLC. 1995.

Schwarz, Joyce. *The Vision Board: The Secret to an Extraordinary Life*. New York, NY: HarperCollins, 2008.

Wattles, Wallace D. *The Science of Getting Rich*. Scottsdale, AZ: LifeSuccess Productions, 1996.

Memory

Beck, Martha. *How to Tune in to the Voice Within*. O, The Oprah Magazine. July 12, 2011.

Benson, Herbert. *The Relaxation Response*. New York, NY: Harper Collins. 2008.

Cahill, Larry and James McCaugh. *Mechanisms of emotional arousal and lasting declarative memory*. Trends in Neuroscience.1998, Vol. 21, No. 7: 294-299.

Craig, Gary. *The EFT Manual*. Santa Rosa, CA: Energy Psychology Press. 2011.

Dispenza, Joe. *Breaking the Habit of Being Yourself*. Carlsbad, CA: Hay House. 2012.

Goldsmith, Timothy H. *How Birds See*. Scientific American., July 2006, pp. 69-75.

Gladstone, William, Richard Greninger and John Selby. *Tapping the Source: Using the Master Key System for Abundance and Happiness*. New York, NY: Sterling Ethos. 2010.

Goleman, Daniel. *Emotional Intelligence: Why It Can Matter More than IQ*. New York, NY: Bantam Books.1995.

Haanel, Charles. *The Master Key System*. Edited by Anthony R. Michalski. Wilkes-Barre, PA.: Kallisti Publishing. 2000.

Hannaford, Carla. *Playing in the Unified Field: Raising & becoming conscious, creative human beings.* Great River Books, Salt Lake City, UT, 2010.

Harris, Russ. *The Confidence Gap: A Guide to Overcoming Fear and Self-Doubt.* Boston, MA: Trumpeter Books. 2011.

Kabat-Zinn, Jon. *Wherever You Go, There You Are: Mindfulness meditation in everyday life.* New York, NY: Hyperion. 2005.

Lally, Phillippa, H. van Jaarsveld, H. Potts and J. Wardle. *How are habits formed: Modelling habit formation in the real world.* European Journal of Social Psychology, 2010, 40(6), pp.998-1009.

Levin, Amir. *Unmasking Memory Genes.* Scientific American Mind, June/July 2008, pp. 50-51.

Loftus, E. F. and J.C. Palmer. *Reconstruction of automobile destruction: An example of the interaction between language and memory.* Journal of Verbal Learning and Verbal Behavior, 1974, Vol. 13, pp.585-589.

Ortner, Nick, Jack Canfield. *The Tapping Solution.* The Tapping Solution, LLC. 2009.

Pert, Candace. *The Molecules of Emotion: Why You Feel the Way You Feel.* New York, NY: Simon & Schuster. 1999.

Pribrium, Karl. *Language of the Brain,* Englewood Cliffs, NJ: Prentice Hall. 1971.

Schafe, Glenn E., Karim Nader, Hugh T. Blair and Joseph E. LeDoux. *Memory consolidation of Pavlovian fear conditioning: a cellular and molecular perspective.* Trends in Neurosciences, 2001, Vol.24 (9) Sep 2001, pp. 540-546.

Singer, Michael A. *The Untethered Soul: The journey beyond yourself.* Oakland, CA: New Harbinger Publications. 2007.

Werblin, Frank and Botond Roska. *The Movies in Our Eyes.* Scientific American, April 2007, pp. 73-79.

Reason

Davis, Bob. *The 1.2% Factor*. Ontario, Canada: Motivated Publishing Studios, 2008.

Dicaprio, Nicholas S. *Teorias de la Personalidad*. México City: McGraw-Hill Interamericana de Mexico, S.A. de C.V, 1989.

Hamati, Selwa. *Once Upon a Recession*. CA: 3L Publishing, 2010.

Proctor, Bob. *It's Not About the Money*. Toronto, Canada: Burman Books, Inc, 2009.

Tsan, Miao. *Sólo Usa Esta Mente*. Houston, TX: Bright Sky Press, 2010.

Perception

Allen, James. *As a Man Thinketh*. Radford, VA: Wilder Publications, 2007

Bandler, Richard and John Grinder. *The Structure of Magic*, Vol.1. Palo Alto, CA: Science and Behavior Books, Inc. 1975.

Hall, Kevin. *Aspire*. New York, NY: Harper Collins Publishers, 2010

Hill, Napoleon. *Think & Grow Rich*. Rockville, MD: ARC Manor, 2007

Holliwell, Raymond. Revised Edition 2007-2004. *Working with the Law*. Life Success Productions LLC.

Maltz, Maxwell. *Psycho-Cybernetics*. New York, NY: Prentice-Hall, Inc, 1960

Pinker, Steven. *How the Mind Works*. New York, NY: W.W. Norton & Company, Inc, 1999

Intuition

Dyer, Wayne. *Real Magic*. New York, NY: HarperCollins, 2001.

Hill, Napoleon. *Think and Grow Rich*. Meriden, CT: Ralston Society, 1937.

Kahneman, Daniel. *Thinking, Fast and Slow*. New York, NY: Farrar, Straus & Giroux, 2011.

Mayer, Elizabeth Lloyd. *Extraordinary Knowing: Science, Skepticism, and the Inexplicable Powers of the Human Mind*. New York, NY: Bantam, Bell, 2007.

Proctor, Bob. LifeSuccess Consultant Training. West Palm Beach, FL, October 2010.

Radhakrishnan, Sarvepalli. Philosopher and Former President of India (1962-1967).

Sonia Choquette. *Trust Your Vibes: Secret Tools for Six-Sensory Living*. Carlesbad, CA: Hay House, 2004.

The Will

Pritchett, Price. *You2* . Dallas, TX:Pritchett & Associates. 2007

Troward, Thomas. *The Edinburgh Lectures on Mental Science*. New York, NY: Dodd, Mead, 1904

Wattles, Wallace. *The Science of Getting Rich*, Holyoke, MA: E. Towne Company, 1910